]

James Graham is a playwright and screenwriter. His plays include *This House* (West End, 2016; National Theatre, 2012), which was nominated for the *Evening Standard* and the Olivier Best Play Award; *Privacy* (Public Theater New York, 2016; Donmar Warehouse, 2014); *Monster Raving Loony* (Plymouth Theatre Royal, Soho Theatre, 2016); *The Vote*, which was broadcast live from the Donmar Warehouse on More4 on the night of the general election, 2015; *Finding Neverland* (on Broadway, 2015); *The Angry Brigade* (Paines Plough and Bush Theatre, 2015); *The Whisky Taster* (Bush Theatre, 2010). As Writer in Residence at the Finborough Theatre, his plays have included *The Man* (2010), *Sons of York* (2008) and *Eden's Empire* (2005), winner of the Catherine Johnson Best Play Award.

James Graham

Ink

Bloomsbury Methuen Drama
An imprint of Bloomsbury Publishing Plc

B L O O M S B U R Y
LONDON · OXFORD · NEW YORK · NEW DELHI · SYDNEY

Bloomsbury Methuen Drama
An imprint of Bloomsbury Publishing Plc.
www.bloomsbury.com

50 Bedford Square   1385 Broadway
London WC1B 3DP   New York NY 10018
UK   USA

Bloomsbury is a registered trademark of Bloomsbury Publishing Plc

First published 2017
Reprinted 2017 (twice)

© James Graham, 2017

British Library Cataloguing-in-Publication Data
A catalogue record for this book is available from the British Library.

ISBN: PB: 978-1-3500-5501-8
ePub: 978-1-3500-5502-5
ePDF: 978-1-3500-5500-1

Library of Congress Cataloging-in-Publication Data
A catalog record for this book is available from the Library of Congress

Series: Modern Plays

Cover design: Olivia D'Cruz
Cover image: Bertie Carvel and Richard Coyle
photographed by Nadav Kander © Almeida Theatre

Typeset by Country Setting, Kingsdown, Kent CT14 8ES
Printed and bound in Great Britain

Ink

Ink was first performed at the Almeida Theatre, London, on 17 June 2017 with the following cast and creative team:

Diana/Chrissie	Rachel Caffrey
Rupert Murdoch	Bertie Carvel
Stephanie Rahn	Pearl Chanda
Bench Hand/Host	Oliver Birch
Larry Lamb	Richard Coyle
Sir Alick	Geoffrey Freshwater
Beverley	Jack Holden
Brian McConnell	Justin Salinger
Hugh Cudlipp	David Schofield
Joyce Hopkirk	Sophie Stanton
Bernard Shrimsley	Tim Steed
Frank Nicklin	Tony Turner
Ray Mills/Lee Howard	Rene Zagger

Writer   James Graham
Director   Rupert Goold
Designer   Bunny Christie
Lighting   Neil Austin
Sound and Composition   Adam Cork
Video   Jon Driscoll
Choreography and Movement Direction   Lynne Page
Casting   Anne McNulty CDG
Resident Director   Rebecca Frecknall
Costume Supervision   Deborah Andrews
Voice and Dialect Coach   Elspeth Morrison
Associate Director   Rebecca Frecknall

Please note that the text of the play which appears in this volume may be changed during the rehearsal process and appear in a slightly altered form in performance.

Characters

Larry Lamb, *forties, Yorkshire: new editor of the* Sun
Rupert Murdoch, *thirties, Australian: owner of the* Sun
Hugh Cudlipp, *fifties, Welsh: editor of the* Mirror
Stephanie Rahn, *twenties, London: model*

An ensemble can play the following team of reporters and other occupants of the Street. Possibly the minimum number required for the ensemble is eight, but equally possibly not.

Brian McConnell	Christopher Timothy
Joyce Hopkirk	Chrissie
Sir Alick McKay	Peter Wilson
Bernard Shrimsley	Rees-Mogg
Beverley Goodway	Hetherington
Lee Howard	Brittenden
Frank Nicklin	Chapel Father
Percy Roberts	Apprentice Printer
Muriel McKay	Bench Hand
Ray Mills	Hosein Brothers
Diana	Typesetters, Stone Hands,
Anna Murdoch	Printers, Messengers
Vic Mayhew	TV Host
John Desborough	CID Commander

Setting

Fleet Street, 1969–70.

Prologue

Darkness at first.

Murdoch   OK, listen – you listening?

Lamb   Yes.

Murdoch   Good, 'cause I want to tell you a story. And it's true. That's what makes it a good fucking story, right, 'cause all the best stories are true – you don't mind me swearing by the way do you? The odd curse, I should have asked.

Lamb   No –

Murdoch   So a good fucking story only has value if it's 'heard'. Right? And for it to be heard it has to be Told Well. So, you tell me, before I tell you *my* story, you tell me what in your mind . . . what in your mind do I need to tell a good story?

Lamb   Well, I . . . alright, I would venture to / say that –

Murdoch   And don't try to be smart, this isn't a goddamn interview, we're just talking, OK, I'm just interested, what makes a good story? Go.

Lamb   Well it's the five 'W's, isn't it.

Murdoch   Five 'W's.

Lamb   Yeah, the first 'W' is Who.

We see who this is, speaking.

Rupert Murdoch, *late thirties, Australian.* **Larry Lamb**, *early forties, Yorkshireman.*

Lamb   Who is important. 'Who' did this. Take us two, right now, you're – what, uh, um, an Australian businessman.

Murdoch   Right.

Lamb   You own a Sunday newspaper.

Murdoch   Yeah.

Lamb   Me? I edit a newspaper.

Murdoch   Uh-uh.

Lamb   So far, not very interesting.

Murdoch   It's a little interesting, but OK –

Lamb   But it becomes more interesting –

Murdoch   Uh-uh.

Lamb   – when we establish that I'm not the editor of *your* newspaper.

Murdoch   Right.

Lamb   So why would we be meeting? You see? That's – 'curious'.

Murdoch   Yeah.

Lamb   And that's the Second 'W' – What. 'What' are they doing?

Murdoch   Having dinner.

They're at a table.

Lamb   We–ell, that's a little boring, but –

Murdoch   It's not boring, I'm hungry.

Lamb   We're having a, a 'negotiation', that's a little more interesting –

Murdoch   Right, right, OK, a, a, a 'surprise' –

Lamb   A 'secret' –

Murdoch   A *secret*. (*Claps.*) Exactly, I love this. A secret negotiation – *over* dinner, please, I'm starving here.

Lamb   Alright then, third 'W' – Where.

Murdoch   Can I pick?

Lamb   Go for it.

Murdoch   Okay dokey, Savoy Grill.

The Savoy Grill.

Lamb   OK, but, just know then that means − (*Gesturing at some* **Guests** *over his shoulder.*) You're going to see Maurice Green, *Telegraph* editor, having dinner with Bob Edwards, editor of the *People*, at their usual table, right over there −

Murdoch   Oh Jesus, I'd forgotten how bloody predictable this Street is, fine.

The surrounding world disappears again.

Lamb   That's the fourth 'W', When, usually the least important, but in this instance, Saturday night, the Savoy Grill, it's a minefield.

Murdoch   I get it, fine, the Waldorf, then.

The Waldorf. (Different tablecloths etc.)

Lamb (*pointing at other* **Guests**)   OK, but, *Daily Mail* and *Sunday Times*.

Murdoch   Fuck's sake.

It disappears.

Rules restaurant.

Lamb   Do you like Rules?

Murdoch   So long as I'm the one making them.

Lamb   The restaurant, it's the oldest −

Murdoch   I know what bloody Rules is, oldest restaurant in London blah blah, fine, just do it, go.

Waiter *approaches with menus.*

Waiter   Good evening and welcome to Rules. The specials today are −

Murdoch   Yeah yeah, we can see the board, bottle of Chianti, '61. (*To* **Larry**.) You like red? There we go. (*Handing back the menu.*) I'll have the rib eye, rare. Now when I say rare what does that mean, here?

Waiter   For a three-centimetre cut, we normally cook each side for two minutes –

Murdoch   No, too long, half that. Just a quick flash in the pan, in–out, fssh.

Waiter   Our chef will normally recommend –

Murdoch   In fact you know what, just like 'show' the steak to the flame, literally, like that, just hold the little guy in your hands, and point out the flame from across the kitchen, and then – (*Hits the table.*) Straight here. Larry?

Lamb   The lobster, please.

Waiter   Thank you. (*Makes to go.*)

Murdoch   Wait, come back.

Waiter   Sir?

Murdoch   I'll have the lobster too.

Waiter   You want to change your –

Murdoch   Yeah, lobster, lobster sounds good. Wait, shit, the Chianti.

Lamb   That's fine, honestly, I don't –

Murdoch   Right, fuck this, this is a disaster, we're starting again.

Lamb   It's fine –

Murdoch   No FUCK it, I mean it, we're going again. (*At the* **Waiter**.) Not him this time, 'Who', you can change the first 'W', right, 'who'?

Lamb   It's your story.

Murdoch (*at the* **Waiter**) Right, piss off Long Tall Sally,
someone else, someone pretty, if we're doing this, let's fucking −

Waitress (*replacing* **Waiter**) Hi.

Murdoch   Better, good, go.

Waitress   Good evening and welcome to −

Murdoch   Exactly, the 'welcome', and all that. Now, can −

Waitress   The specials are on the board −

Murdoch   Yeah and the shit with the board, OK, good;
we're having the lobster, two of them, and a bottle of the
Pouilly-Fumé, thank you.

She goes.

So what's the fifth? The fifth 'W'?

Lamb   Fifth 'W' I used to think was the most important,
now I think it's the least. Fifth 'W' is Why.

Murdoch   You think the least important question is 'Why',
I would have said that was the most important question.

Lamb   Once you know 'why' something happened, the
story's over, it's dead. Don't answer why, a story can run and
run, can run forever. And the other reason, actually, honestly,
I think, is that there is no 'Why?' Most times. 'Why' suggests
there's a plan, that there is a point to things, when they happen
and there's not, there's just not. Sometimes shit − just −
happens. Only thing worth asking isn't 'Why', it's . . . (*Shrugs.*)
'What next?'

Beat. **Murdoch** *smiles, enjoying this.*

Murdoch   You're in Manchester and you don't want to be.

Lamb   I want to be an editor and there was no openings on
the Street so I left to −

Murdoch   Northern Editor of the *Daily Mail* is not an
editor −

Lamb   Actually it's quite a –

Murdoch   No, let's not fuck around, it's not, you're better than that. You were the best sub on the Street, did your time at the *Mirror* and after a decade it began to dawn on you they would never let you sit in the pilot's seat. Not you. Not the Yorkshire-born son of a blacksmith, not the guy who didn't get a degree from Oxford or Cambridge, who didn't get a degree from anywhere. Not you.

I've bought a newspaper.

Lamb   I know, a Sunday, the *News of the World*.

Murdoch   I bought a *daily* newspaper. I just bought a daily newspaper from your old paper.

Lamb   You bought a paper from the *Mirror*? What are they selling? Oh Jesus. Is it the *People*, tell me it's the *People*.

Murdoch   I have offices –

Lamb   Tell me it's not the –

Murdoch   – and a machine room, rotary presses that don't press anything for six days of the week. I need a daily. I –

Lamb   Tell me it's not the *Sun*.

Murdoch   . . . I've bought the *Sun*.

And.

Lamb   Oh shhh—

Murdoch   I need an editor.

Lamb   Ah bollocks. Is that why you asked me down, to . . . (*Sigh.*) Ah fuck. I thought . . . God, I'm a – I *really* thought this might be my –

Murdoch   Your way back. It still can be.

Lamb   The *Sun* – sorry, Rupert – it's a laughing stock on the Street, a stuck-up broadsheet that has never once made a profit, it's selling less than, what, 850,000 –

Murdoch   800 and falling.

Lamb   Jesus. (*Head in hands.*)

Murdoch   And it doesn't have to be a stuck-up broadsheet – Who – who bloody says it has to stay a stuck-up broadsheet? We could . . . we could 'change' it.

Lamb   Change it. To what?

Murdoch   I dunno, something 'new', a new newspaper.

Lamb   You can't just, just invent a new newspaper and assume –

Murdoch   Why not?

Lamb   – in the same way you, you wouldn't change your football team, the British are . . . we're creatures of habit, and –

Murdoch   I hate that, I hate it. It's ludicrous, everything's so old. In Australia we don't mind new because everything *had* to be new. *We* just have to find a *new* market.

Lamb   There are no new markets.

Murdoch   Bullshit, you're just too afraid to say it, in case the world thinks you're a bloody fool. Well guess what. You're sat opposite the Other Bloody Fool.

It's the same market the paper we're buying it from *used* to serve, but is now failing.

Lamb   The *Mirror*? Faili— it's the biggest selling newspaper in Britain.

Murdoch   It used to be fearless, provocative, *fun* – where's the fun gone from the Street, it's boring, fuck it. It used to speak to the working classes, in the industrial heartlands, the run-down suburbs. And you, I think you know how to make a paper to reach those forgotten people, don't you? Because you *are* one of them – were. Your family, your friends, your neighbours, in your ordinary Yorkshire mining town.

What's your father's paper, what does he read?

Lamb   He re— He *used* to read the *Mirror*.

Murdoch   See, *used* to – exactly. What does he read now?

Lamb   Nothing, he's dead.

Murdoch (*beat*)   We try harder to please them when they're gone, don't we? Funny.

So give him a paper, Larry. Make a paper for him. The family he left behind –

Lamb   Alright, you don't . . . I don't need you to romanticise my 'eeh bah gum' Yorkshire past, yes of course I see the, the shit that's dumped off the presses now, telling people what they *should* be interested in, rather than reflecting *who* they really are, yes, fine. But how do you expect to reach them with a brand-new paper they've never heard of? It isn't possible.

Murdoch   You just said it. Stop giving them what you think they need, start offering them what they want. A popular paper, for the masses. One that can 'unleash' a part of us, a part of the British character that I think, humbly speaking, has never been tapped into, but is there, yearning for stuff. Maybe it takes an outsider to see it.

Lamb   The *Mirror* . . . These are my people, you're asking me / to go against

Murdoch   Oh bugger off, 'your' people. Larry . . .

Lamb   The Street has given me / a lot of opportunities, and I don't want to –

Murdoch   No, all it's done is take from you, Larry, *listen* to me. I said I had a story for you. An exclusive. Never been told. And the story is true. The headline is –

The headline is visually typed and set somewhere for us . . .

SHOCKING BRITISH CONSPIRACY

What's the main picture? The picture is –

A flash bulb picks out – a new scene, separate from them.

Men, *meeting, shaking hands with each other.*

At this point, perhaps **Murdoch** *leaves the table, joining the scene. Perhaps* **Lamb** *joins him, watching, as they tread around the action that is being described, invisible observers.*

Murdoch   A little under a year ago, there was a clandestine meeting between the most powerful *unelected* men in the country. (*Referencing.*) Here? Cecil King – chairman of the *Mirror*. Best-selling paper. Who's he shaking hands with? Go on, for ten points?

Another flash bulb pops, capturing the changing scene, each time revealing a new handshake.

Lamb   That's Lord Mountbatten.

Murdoch   Bingo. Highest ranking officer in the military. This, this is Solly Zuckerman – he's only the bloody fella with the British nuclear codes.

Lamb   I know who Solly Zuckerman is.

Murdoch   It's his finger on the button. And this fella here, I assume you know . . .

Lamb *walks close to the guy in question. A moment . . .*

Lamb   Yeah. I know this fella.

Murdoch   Hugh Cudlipp. The editor of the *Mirror*. Your dear friend –

Lamb   *Old* friend. What do they want?

Murdoch   To overthrow the government.

Lamb   . . . What?

Murdoch   Yup. Bring down Wilson, his high spending, the national debt, all that.

Lamb   The *Mirror*'s a Labour-supporting paper –

Murdoch   Exactly. See? Oh I know, I know you bought into the whole philosophy, the 'values' the *Mirror* claims to stand for, democracy, freedoms, the emancipation of working people, well, behold, the hypocrisy of your treasured, *liberal*, establishment. The belief that they know best, that it's their, what, 'responsibility' to reverse the poor democratic choices of the people they pretend to defend. And replace the government with their own committee, led by Mountbatten. A military coup.

Lamb   I . . . I was – come on, I was there, at this time, at the *Mirror*, you think I wouldn't have known the executives were plotting a – I was part of this circle.

Murdoch   And yet funnily enough – you aren't in the picture.

Lamb   . . .

Murdoch   Your people, Larry. There to hold power to account; always happens, as sure as the sun replaces the moon, the revolutionaries become the very elites they overthrew.

Lamb   So publish. If it's true, you'll destroy them –

Murdoch   Number one, the coup didn't happen, was never realistically going to happen, it was insane, born of a sickness that has grown deep inside the whole system. And number two . . . there are other ways to destroy people.

(*At* **Hugh Cudlipp**.) The man standing quietly in the corner knew that. Saw that his mentor, King, the man who had raised him up, championed him, saw that he'd finally tipped over the edge of reason. And now it was his chance to grab power for himself.

Lamb   I knew the board rolled over on to King, I had no idea it was Hugh who did the pushing. I'm almost impressed; didn't know he had it in him.

Murdoch   King is now just the latest in a long line of fallen barons, names you can hear to this day on the wind as it whistles down the Street. 'Beaverbrook'. 'Northcliffe'. 'Rothermere'.

Lamb   And one day . . . 'Murdoch'?

Murdoch   The moral of this story is . . . that power replaces itself with itself. And you can either stand on the other side of the window, tap tap tap, asking to come in. Or, you establish . . . a *new* line of ascension.

(*Looks at* **Lamb**, *checks his watch.*) Walk with me. The Street. It's Saturday night –

Lamb   I've seen the Street on a Saturday night –

Murdoch   My presses will be starting up in the *News of the World* basement. Given that currently only happens once a week, I like to be there when they do. Come on . . .

Fleet Street. At night.

The lit-up signs from different press houses.

The Daily Telegraph. *The* Express. *The* Daily Mail. *The* Mirror. *The* Guardian.

The lights from the machine rooms in basements kick into life, running their presses.

The silhouettes of the **Bench Hands** *tossing the bundle stacks of papers from one to the other.*

Lamb *and* **Murdoch** *passing through, to . . .*

The News of the World *– and soon, the* Sun.

An office. **Murdoch** *pours them a drink.*

Lamb (*looking around*)   Jesus . . .

Murdoch   Yeah. But I like to think little imperfections give things a certain 'character'. Like that little birthmark on your forehead –

Lamb   It's not a birthmark. It's a scar.

Murdoch   Really? How'd you get it? In a fight?

Lamb   Rupert . . . I get that you've come here, ready to, to take everything on, but I know what I'm talking about. The Street really is the Wild West. It'll stand on you and crush you and keep crushing, just because you tried.

Murdoch   Oh, you think I've not had to roll my sleeves up before? Punch my way out of corners? You think I'm afraid of these old bastards? I throw everything I have into this Sunday rag, to 'buy my way in', finally. My first time in the old Press Club? All the other chairmen in their leather chairs, clutching their papers, what happens? Up they go – (*Demonstrates lifting a paper over his face.*) Not one handshake. No cigar. Nothing. 'The Aussie sheep farmer'. Well not for much longer, eh?

Lamb   So that's what this is. Revenge.

Murdoch   No. It's business. And it's revenge.

I'm giving you the chance they never did, and it's your *last* chance. I don't mean to be the cunt that points that out, but there you go.

(*Gesturing.*) Captain of your own ship. It's not much, but it could be yours. I sign the papers tomorrow, tick-tock. What do you say? Me and you together, Larry. Rupert the Sheep, and Larry the Lamb.

Lamb   . . .

A slow rumble begins to rise from beneath them.

Murdoch   Listen. They're starting . . .

Feel that . . . ?

What do you say?

Lamb *looks around the place. Beat . . .*

Lamb   There'll be a lot of blood.

Murdoch   God. I hope so.

The presses beneath are winding up violently, louder and louder, the furniture in the office beginning to shake, as the sound becomes deafening.

A new headline, typed into view over the pounding noise.

PAGE ONE

Act One

The Chairman's office at the Mirror.

Lamb *and* **Murdoch**, *along with* **Sir Alick McKay**, *are greeted by Mirror chairman* **Hugh Cudlipp** *and its editor* **Lee Howard**.

On the wall – a chart, with different coloured strings, showing sales. The Mirror *leading in red,* Sun *bottom in yellow.*

Cudlipp   Larry. Been a long time. How's the north?

Lamb   Uh, the weather's colder but the people are warmer, so, evens out.

Cudlipp   You know Lee Howard from your time here, our new senior editor.

Lamb   Yeah, I knew you made Lee editor . . . Alright, Lee.

Murdoch   Sir Alick McKay, my deputy chairman.

Sir Alick   Yes, we all met, during the talks, hello again, how do.

Murdoch   Right, is that enough foreplay, can we get down to the fucking?

Cudlipp *(beat, then)*   You know, I once had dealings with your father. When we opened the *Melbourne Argos* as a joint venture. I liked him.

Murdoch   Good. I liked him.

Cudlipp   He – *(Chuckling a little, at* **Lee**.*)* I remember over dinner actually, him saying to me once how, at the time, he was worried about 'his boy Rupert'. Worried he hadn't found his, his – path, yet. I never imagined I'd be standing opposite the boy himself one day, selling him a newspaper.

Murdoch *(beat, open hands)*   The webs we weave, Hugh.

Cudlipp (*a piece of paper*)   The agreement, all signed off by the board.

Sir Alick   May I? (*Taking it, glasses on.*) Ta so much.

Lamb   What's happening to the current staff?

Cudlipp   We'll be absorbing most of them back into the *Mirror*, we have –

Lamb   And the rest?

Cudlipp   They're yours to interview and/or make redundant as you /see –

Lamb   So, you'll be taking all the good ones.

Cudlipp   They're all a high calibre, you know that. We're looking at Saturday 15th November, our final edition. Then, Monday morning, the *Sun*'s 'name' and whatever staff we don't keep – all yours. (*With the contract.*) All for . . . £1.75 million.

Lamb   Well, we obviously won't be going to print on that Monday after your Saturday edition, we'll need months to being prepping our new ideas –

Cudlipp   Ah. Yes. No, sorry. That's . . . (*Pushing forward the contract.*) One of the stipulations. When my predeces— (*A brief, guilty glance at the* **King** *portrait.*) When *we* bought the title in '64 we had to make the old owners two assurances. That the *Sun* would be always be a Labour supporting paper – now, OK, we've said, to facilitate a quick sale, that that's one of the assurances, under your objection, they are happy to drop.

Sir Alick   Which is appreciated, naturally, but –

Murdoch   And the other?

Cudlipp   The second assurance *isn't* negotiable. That there must be five years of *continual* publication. It was important to the family that the title last. So –

Lamb   You bought it in 1964? So, it's '69, that's five years, done.

Cudlipp   *December* '64. So just shy, by a matter of weeks. Sorry. So, no, there can be no break. You'll have a little over one day to turn around your new paper.

A moment.

Lamb   That's not / possible –

Murdoch (*taking the contract*)   We'll do it.

Lamb   Mr Murdoch, / just a – we –

Murdoch   Yeah, how hard can it be, we can't make it worse than it already is, can we? – I mean, that with all due respect, Hugh. You print *your* final *Sun* on Saturday, we'll print our entirely new paper for Monday. Do you have a pen?

Cudlipp   . . . An 'entirely *new*' paper? I'd have thought – 'continuity', for a time, was the only realistic possibility. As I think Larry was about to say, it / isn't possible –

Lamb   No, don't worry, we'll turn something around. Go ahead, Mr Murdoch.

Lee   Actually, we've arranged a little, sort of, signing 'ceremony', in the boardroom, if you don't –

Murdoch   No, you're alright.

Lee   There's brandy and some 'snacks'.

Murdoch   Alright, chuck the snacks, but we'll choke down the booze. Alick?

Cudlipp   I'll be right with you.

Murdoch, **Sir Alick** *and* **Lee** *exit into the other room, leaving* **Lamb** *and* **Cudlipp** *alone.*

Cudlipp   How's the family? The girls?

Lamb   . . . Well, ta, thank you. Joan sends her love.

Cudlipp   As does Jodi. She was a little surprised, when I told her.

Larry, what is this? If you wanted a job that badly –

Lamb   I had a job, and now I have a new job, this –

Cudlipp   Why do you think I'm selling it? Why do you think I'm selling it so *cheap*, instead of just closing the blasted thing.

Lamb   You couldn't close it, that many job losses, the unions would halt production of your entire publishing stock; don't talk to me like I'm the copy boy, Hugh, like I wasn't on the team, I slaved every night on that subs' desk, over every line, word, comma, fucking colon. I helped build the *Mirror* into what it is, don't think I can't take what I know and go do it somewhere else, somewhere better.

Cudlipp   Ah yes, right, with your – what did you call them, your 'new' ideas. Incredible, for such an old trade, for you to have discovered something brand-new that none of us have before.

Come back, Larry. Why don't you come back on to the team. Come *home*.

Lamb   . . . I can't. I'm the editor of my own newspaper now –

Cudlipp   Edit one of mine, pick one.

Lamb   You're lying, just trying to –

Cudlipp   I'm serious.

Lamb *wavers momentarily, looking next door where* **Murdoch** *is . . .*

Cudlipp   I'm serious, pick one.

Lamb   . . . The *Mirror*.

Cudlipp   We print more than just the *Mirror*, Larry.

Lamb   I know. Sounds like you might be over-extending yourself, Hugh. I mean, look at the *Sun*. That's a right pile of crap, that is.

Murdoch *and* **Sir Alick** *return, a brandy in hand.*

Murdoch   Right, that's all official then. Shall we?

Cudlipp   Wait, we should have the traditional photo, shouldn't we? All together, shaking hands, a nice symbol for the Street —

Lee (*leaning in*)   Hugh? Percy asked for a quick hello.

Cudlipp   . . . Forgive me, one moment.

He exits with **Lee**, *leaving the three intruders in his office alone.*

Murdoch   'Signing ceremonies', photos, fuck's sake. These pompous arses.

Sir Alick (*at his glass*)   Brandy's not much cock, either, worse luck.

Lamb   No dummy runs? Less than — (*Checks his watch.*) A matter of *weeks* until the handover and then a *one*-day turnaround, are you *fucki*—

Sir Alick   Oy, Larry, language, good heavens!

Lamb   With a skeleton staff of their effing rejects, and then hahaha, which ever loser hacks you think I'd be able to poach from other papers to work under *these* conditions . . .

Murdoch   I poached you, didn't I? Find people like you. The spurned, the spited, the overlooked; gather 'em up, throw 'em in. A ship of undesirables.

Sir Alick   You have a payroll big enough for a hundred people. No more.

Lamb   The *Mirror* have four hundred.

Murdoch   They're over-staffed.

Lamb   Rupert —

Murdoch   Larry. What did he say to you? Try to tempt you back? Oy, I'd be disappointed if he didn't.

He sneaks over to **Cudlipp**'s *chair, checks the coast is clear, and sits in it, spinning – him and* **Sir Alick** *laughing, as* **Murdoch** *looks around his desk and drawers.*

Murdoch   Look at him, master and commander, of all he surveys.

He stands and imitates wanking over the papers on the desk.

Masturbating all over the faces of the grateful British public, 'Oh Mr Cudlipp, Mr Cudlipp, thank you!'

Sir Alick   Oh Rupert, honestly, do you mind?!

Murdoch   Well. Radical thought. But I'm going to run my paper – like it's a *business*. (*Mock-gasps.*) Not a public service. Not an educational programme. Not a church. Margins, bottom lines, the figures are what counts. In fact . . .

He sees the circulation chart with coloured strings, and approaches it. The Sun *figures in yellow.*

Wouldn't it be so bloody satisfying . . . if this line (*yellow string*), overtook this line (*red string*) . . . within one year. Twelve months from the day of our launch.

Lamb   One of the lowest-selling papers in the country overtaking the biggest-selling paper in the world.

Murdoch   Yeahhhhh. Wouldn't that be a good '*story*'.

Lamb   Is it an ultimatum? A / condition of my –

Murdoch   No, it's a target, and a bit of fun.

Lamb   Need I remind you I haven't signed any contract yet. I could just walk.

Murdoch   I do believe you're right. Alick?

Sir Alick (*taking a contract out from his jacket*)   Very healthy expense account, as you'll see, car complete with driver, and this as your salary.

Lamb   . . . I won't be 'managed', needing your say-so on every hire.

Murdoch *takes a fancy pen on a stand from* **Cudlipp**'*s desk. And holds it out for* **Lamb**.

Murdoch   Make the paper you want, I trust you.

Lamb *signs his contract. He's about to replace the pen . . . but puts it inside his own pocket instead.*

Murdoch   I just want something . . . 'loud'.

A Fleet Street cabaret club.

Stephanie Rahn *steps into the lights . . .*

She is twenty-one, of mixed British and Indian origin. Joined by other female **Singers** *as a* **Band** *kicks in.*

They sing or play under the following sequence, as –

Lamb *bounces around the different iconic bars, pubs and clubs, rounding up his new team.*

There could be a dance element to this movement too as we turn from one into the other . . .

El Vino's restaurant and bar.

A **Landlady** *spotting* **Lamb** *pass through –*

Landlady   Bloody hell, Larry! The prodigal son returns. I thought you'd died.

Lamb   No – well, inside a bit, maybe. Not seen McConnell around, have yer?

Landlady   What, Brian, that bastard? Got barred from El Vino's. You could try the Stab?

The Stab in the Back — a spit and sawdust pub.

John Desborough *singing along in the pub to the song, as other* **Journalists** *join in.* **Lamb** *leans over the piano . . .*

John *stops singing momentarily, but keeps playing under.*

John   Stone me, Larry Lamb's looking over me piano!

Some other **Journalists** *cheer him — possibly mockingly.*

Lamb   John. You've not seen McConnell about?

John   That old gobshite? Got barred from the Stab. You tried the Tip?

Lamb *nods his thanks. Makes to go. Doesn't . . .*

Lamb   You're still political at the *Mirror*?

John   Senior Political Editor, if you please. (*Downs his pint.*)

Lamb   Fancy a change?

John (*laughs*)   What? To Rupert's 'Shit Sheet'? I'm alright, thank you!

He laughs, hard. As do others . . .

As the band swells again, **Lamb** *exits, into the Street. He lights a fag.*

Checks his watch. An idea . . .

He begins to strip his clothes off, stepping into —

The Fleet Street Turkish Baths.

Lamb   Hello, Brian.

Brian McConnell *is laid down in the water, a fag in his mouth still.*

Brian   Who's that, can't see through the steam.

Lamb   The Ghost of Christmas Past. (*Gets into the water.*)

Brian   As I live and breathe. (*Coughs, smokes.*)

Lamb   Sounds like breathing doesn't come all that easy any more, Bri.

Brian   'S alright, this steam, it helps open up the lungs. (*Tugs again on his fag.*) How'd you find me?

Lamb   Heard you'd been in the Tip till five a.m., no time to go home, knew you'd shit, shower and shave here. Not much changes on the Street.

Brian   I dunno. Apparently some things do.

Lamb   I have some news.

Brian   Yeah well, that's the business we're in.

(*Smokes.*) Shouldn't be here. I'm seen talking to you, they'll have me out on my arse –

Lamb   I've accepted it. The position.

Brian   And what position's that, down on all fours, mouth open? You're an idiot, Larry, which is strange, because you're the smartest bugger I know. What does Joan think?

Lamb   Joan thinks . . . Joan'll come round. Look, Brian –

Brian   Please don't ask me, Larry. It ain't fair. I can't say no to you, and you know that, so I'm asking you not to ask, alright?

They both stand as the music swells again, towels whipped on, as –

The locker room, afterwards.

Lamb *and* **Brian**

Brian   News editor?!

Lamb   Shh, keep your fucking –

Brian   I'm not senior management, Larry, I'm a hack –

Lamb   You mean no one's given you a chance.

Brian   Why would I leave the best newspaper on the Street?

Lamb   Because it isn't the best any more.

Brian (*looking around him, aware of listening ears*)   I happen to believe, Mr Lamb, that the *Mirror* is the crown jewel of Fleet Street, and a bastion of journalistic –

Lamb   Cut the shit, no one's listening, and you know full well how stuck up its own arse it's become, Jesus.

Brian   Hugh Cudlipp's not stuck up. He's Welsh.

Lamb   You can be posh and Welsh, Bri.

Brian   No you can't, name one.

Lamb   . . . Prince of Wales.

Beat. **Brian** *smiles, a bit . . .*

Brian   I'm a crime writer, bloody *crime*. What do I know about editing the news?

Lamb   News the *Mirror* way? Probably nothing, but what if we treated the news as *if* it were a crime thriller, a mystery! Plot twists, whodunnits! An entertaining page-turner that slaps you in the face rather than sends you to sleep.

Brian   That's what he wants, is it?

Lamb   That's what *I* want. Have done for years, what *we* always talked about, propping up the bar of the Tip for all those years – our *own* paper.

Brian   I'm settled, now.

Lamb   You're bored, now.

Brian   Course I'm bored, everyone's bored. Is this just about proving a point?

Lamb . . . Really? That just got said, did it, me?

Brian Well then, why?

Lamb Least important question, Bri, did I not teach you that?

Brian Why 'me'?

Lamb Because I *know* you. And you know me. You can be a sort of . . . 'grounding', influence, on me. My 'perspective'.

Brian What, tell you when you're getting too big for your boots?

Lamb If you like –

Brian Larry, you're getting too big for your boots –

Lamb Brian. (*Hand out.*) Come on.

Brian (*sighs*) You'll not bring anyone else with you, you know that.

They both stand, **Brian** *part of the 'dance' now, as he spins into* –

Brian *in The Mucky Duck.*

Vic Mayhew *is greeted by* **Brian**.

Brian Vic Mayhew! The best sub-editor on the street. Drink!

Vic Answer's no, Bri.

Brian Oh.

Vic Yeah sorry.

Brian Right.

Vic So.

Brian Whisky, anyway?

Vic Won't make a difference.

Brian   Fair enough, how d'you like it?

Vic   Massive.

As they move between pubs –

Brian (*tapping*)   Let's go for Ray Mills next, he's a brute, and we're gonna need brute force for this –

The Printer's Devil

With **Ray Mills** *– a thuggish, frightening sub. He's playing darts.*

They all down copious amounts of beer as they talk.

Ray   Oy, you pair – respectfully, Mr Lamb, Printer's Devil is for subs. Editors go to the hifalutin Press Club, and crime writ— Well, I've no idea where you go, Brian, honest to God, but traditions need respecting –

Lamb   Ray, when Hugh sells us the *Sun*, he's not moving you to the *Mirror*.

But. We'd like you to sub-edit our *Sun*.

Go on, just swallow it.

Ray *downs his drink.*

Lamb   I meant your pride.

Ray   I know what you meant. Why me?

Lamb   Our writers, stone hands, block makers . . . we're going to be putting them all under some pretty tough conditions. The sub is the centre of a paper's gravity. You're an ex-docker, union man. People would follow you. You would – charm 'em.

Ray   I've never been called charming before. What other posts need filling?

Lamb   Nearly all of 'em. Actually, all of 'em.

Ray   When for?

Lamb   Five weeks.

Ray   Not long enough.

Lamb   We know.

Ray   How much money you got?

Brian   Hardly any.

Ray   What's your criteria?

Lamb   Anyone who says 'yes'.

Ray   Does it matter if they've been sacked, arrested, or both?

Lamb   Not in the slightest.

Ray   Alright, get your pad out.

The White Swan.

Frank Nicklin, *fifties, with* **Lamb**.

Brian   So, Frank, you were assistant sports editor at the old *Sun*?

Frank   Yeah, and I heard Cudlipp's not moving me back to the *Mirror*. And you no doubt want someone younger, fresher-faced for yer new *Sun*, eh? So. Looks like paid redundancy for me then, eh? Retirement. Oh well. It's fine. I understand.

Lamb (*handing him a contract*)   We'd like you to be our sports editor –

Frank   Awh FUCK!

Lamb   I know, mate, bad luck, sorry.

Frank   I had plans. I was going to play golf.

Lamb   So, Frank, here's the deal –

Frank   Shit the bed.

Lamb   We don't have any presses outside London, so, in order to get our first editions on the trains up north . . . our print deadline is a bit earlier than other papers.

Frank   How much earlier?

Lamb   8.10 p.m.

Frank   So that means –

Lamb   – we'll never be able to carry footie scores, no.

Frank   No footie scores?! Are you mad?

Lamb   No, we're going to have to use our . . . 'imaginations', to come up with . . . 'something else'. Stories.

Frank   Stories, what do you mean 'stories'?

Lamb   Look, respectfully, you don't have a choice. And also, I don't know, it could be . . . (*Thinks.*) 'Fun'.

Frank (*consider this, takes a sip*)   Hmm. 'Fun', eh . . .

El Vino's.

Lamb *approaches* **Joyce Hopkirk**, *smoking at her table.*

Lamb   Mrs Hopkirk, my name's –

Joyce   Who else?

Lamb   I'm sorry?

Joyce   Who else did you try before me; the answer's 'no', by the way.

Lamb   You're the first.

Joyce   Carefully, you nearly had my eye out then, Pinocchio.

Lamb (*sitting, sincere*)   Joyce. You're the first.

I've heard the rumours, the talk, writers on the *Mirror*'s women's pages not being happy with the direction of –

Joyce   Not happy? (*Aware of the nearby drinkers.*) The *Mirror*, Mr Lamb, happens to be the finest example / of journalism –

Lamb   Of journalistic integrity, 'crown jewel of the Street', yes I know. What do you really think?

Joyce   What do I really think? . . . That since I joined it's become stuffy and dowdy and *old*, you already knew that, but it's also got five million readers and you've got –

Lamb   What I'm offering is the opposite. We want to represent real women, not as seen through the squeamish eyes of Hugh Cudlipp, but –

Joyce   Really? You and Mr Murdoch are secret feminists, are you, *that's* why you're buying this newspaper?

Lamb   I'm saying I think we could give women a voice. That through writers like you, Joyce, we could champion the cause of modern women –

Joyce   I don't want to champion the cause of modern women –

Lamb   Well, I mean to do –

Joyce   I mean I do, of course, but I want to do that by championing the cause of me. Make me woman's editor. Not just a features writer.

Lamb (*smiles*)   That's exactly the role I had in mind.

Joyce   Really?

Lamb   Yep.

Joyce   What happens if I fuck it up?

Lamb   I'd fire you, Joyce.

He winks and exits one way . . .

Fleet Street sandwich shop.

Lamb *and* **Brian** *with* **Bernard Shrimsley** – *lean and smart, straight posture and tight tie* – *standing at a high counter eating sandwiches and drinking coffee.*

Brian (*at his coffee*)   Jesus, what's that?

Lamb   It's coffee, Brian, like a black Russian without the vodka.

Brian   Can't we just go over to the Tip?

Bernard   Sorry, rule of thumb, I don't drink with hacks, compromises the job.

Lamb   Thanks for coming down on the train, Bernard, we really –

Bernard   Cut to it, let me guess, you're having to scrape the figurative bottom of the proverbial barrel – the 'provincial' barrel, no less. Manchester, Sheffield, Leeds?

Lamb   Are you enjoying life at the *Liverpool Post*, Bernard?

Bernard   No, I hate it.

Lamb   We're looking for someone with experience.

Bernard   Is that a euphemism for old fart?

Lamb   Do you want to be our deputy editor?

Bernard   Alright.

Lamb   . . . Really?

Bernard   Yeah, fine then. I should warn you that nobody likes me.

Lamb   That's alright, nobody's ever liked me particularly much either –

Bernard   I am incredibly particular when it comes to layout and I have exacting standards that I will not be lowering for – well, for whatever low standards I hear are in the offing from your new proprietor.

Lamb   Of course. Wouldn't dream of it . . . (*Wincing privately at* **Brian**.)

Brian   Last up, some photographer. Never heard of her, 'Beverley' . . . twenty-five.

They both look 'intrigued' by the prospect of meeting this young woman, stepping into –

The Golden Egg café.

Beverley Goodway, *twenties, holding a camera.*

Brian   You're a fella.

Beverley   Yes.

Brian   You're called Beverley, we – we thought you were a bird.

Beverley   No. Sorry.

Brian (*sighs*)   Do you have a portfolio, or – ?

Beverley   Oh, I – I'm only just getting started, really. Background's more in medicine. Used to take photos in the mortuary, you know. Dead bodies.

Lamb   And now you're on the sports desk at *The Times*.

Beverley   Yeah, I think they're going to fire me, soon. Everything goes so fast, keep missing goals and things. Dead bodies, you can, you know / take your time.

Brian   Take your time. Right.

Beverley   What are you looking to shoot?

Brian   Anything. Stock pictures. Women, quite a lot. Girls.

Beverley   Girls? What will they be doing?

Brian   Standing, wearing things, sometimes not a lot of things. Pointing at things and, you know, like laughing and stuff.

Beverley   'Not a lot of things', you mean like – naked?

Lamb   What, no, of course not fucking naked, Jesus. Just like – bras and pants and stuff, the usual. 'Tasteful'. We might be planning to slaughter a great many sacred cows but no one's going to go that far. This is fucking England after all.

Brian   Where there hardly is any fucking. Least in my experience.

Beverley   Sounds like a no-brainer, all this, doesn't it.

Brian   Yeah.

Beverley   So why are me hands shaking?

Lamb (*pen and contract*)   Are they steady enough to sign this?

Beverley (*taking the pen*) Give it a whirl, yeah.

He signs and steps away as **Lamb** *and* **Brian** *look at their completed list – with some doubt – but nevertheless shake hands. It's a start . . .*

Bang, bang, bang – heavy overhanging lights turn on one by one in the Sun *offices, illuminating –*

The newsroom . . .

Lamb *steps forward as staff assemble.*

Lamb   Uh, hello. Erm –

Ray   All o' yer, quiet, now!

Lamb   . . . Thank you. To some of you, this is hello, welcome. To many of you from the old *Sun* . . . this is goodbye.

And as you'll know it's a tradition on this Street, to send you out a certain way, and that is something we'll honour now. So to those leaving – everyone?

A thumping of fists on desks begins, growing. Bang, bang, bang . . . as a pack of reporters gathered together, looking around, mixed emotions, begin to drift away as one to the building thunder.

The horseshoe subs' desk, other metal tables scattered around, with typewriters, phones with cables that hang down from the ceilings, and on each a spike – a sharp metal stick – where cut stories are 'spiked'.

Lamb, **Brian** *with* **Bernard**, **Ray**, **Frank** *and* **Joyce**, *though more activity on the floor around them.* **Bernard** *has his layout pad on display. Another flip chart. '21 Days to Launch'.*

From now on, it should go without saying, that an insane amount of alcohol is drunk, by everyone, at any time of day. Whisky, beer, gin. And smoking constantly.

Lamb   Alright, amongst everything else – (*Phone rings, he answers.*) Not now. (*Puts it down.*) If we're turning this into a tabloid layout, the print room boys need to reconfigure the presses almost immediately, so –

Brian   Aah! Sorry, think I just saw a rat.

Joyce   Oh give over, what's it gonna do to you?

Brian   God, this fucking place . . .

Lamb   Time to shine, Bernard, go.

Bernard *sketching, turning pages continually.*

Bernard   So – convention nowadays is justified alignments and equal spacing, everything clean and clear. These are some recent, very successful, *Mirror* front pages.

Holding some front pages from 1969. The Kray Twins are sentenced . . . Man walks on the Moon.

Lamb   Right, lacking in attitude or character whatsoever but hey-ho.

Bernard (*drawing*)   So, at Mr Lamb's request . . . ours, at least, could use a bigger logo. And, we could use – (*Sighs.*) 'Fun' items, such as starbursts for offers, say, and bubbles for listings, and such.

Lamb   Bernard. You're a good man, the best at what you do. But more. Fucking more, mate. More bastards and bangers and screamers.

Bernard (*sighs*)   Right, well, it's not a children's comic, unless it is / but –

Joyce   I know I'm setting you all up for an easy one here but what's a bastard?

Ray   Different column inches and widths, no, like, conformity.

Bernard   It's when they're not justified – literally, *and* figuratively.

Lamb   I want it to, to 'jump' out at me, be surprising.

Bernard   Well, ugly is surprising, I'll grant you that.

Lamb   Well, maybe, maybe we need a bit of ugly, this country, maybe it's time. We only get one shot to launch, and we are deeply under-resourced, let's turn that into our virtue. Headlines – underlined, and in some cases overlined. Huge fonts, and half of it italicised.

Bernard   Oh for goodness' – you're basically asking our paper to slouch!

Lamb   No, lean forward. With momentum. It's – like, it's – 'optimistic'!

Bernard   By what degree, italicised?

Lamb   Thirty?

Bernard / Frank   Thirty?!

Bernard   Did we lose the bloody war?! Eighty, best offer.

Lamb   Sixty, it's not a slouch, it's an elegant lean. Gene Kelly in *Singing in the Rain*, like . . .

He demonstrates a rough sixty-degree lean, against the wall.

Bernard   . . . Seventy degrees.

Beat. **Lamb** *readjusts his lean up a bit and looks at* **Brian***, who nods.*

Lamb   Alright, done.

Ray   These are from Hobson Bates. Options for the masthead logo.

Which? Any of them?

Lamb   I dunno, they're all a bit . . . I dunno.

Joyce   . . . 'Fussy'.

Lamb   Yeah, they're –

Bernard   This is the best ad agency in London.

Lamb   Yeah, and it shows. We want something . . . I dunno.

Taking a piece of paper, opening his bag, searching. He's found a child's pencil case.

Brian   The hell is that?

Lamb   Daughter's pencil case, must have took it by mistake (*Takes a random felt tip pen – it's red.*) I don't know, something . . .

Larry *places his design for the logo on the projector. Near to the* Sun *logo we recognise.*

Lamb   Frank, what does that look like?

Frank   Like *you* just drew it.

Lamb   Perfect.

Bernard   You're kid— These things last, Mr Lamb.

Lamb   It's decided.

Frank   And, sorry to bring, you know, logistics and practicalities into this otherwise very entertaining theoretical discussion, but how are we meant to get stories when we don't have any staff, a team this size?

Lamb   Find a way, work from the wires, pad things out.

Brian   Pad things out? He's only used to writing Leyton Orient, 3 – Derby County, 2, eh Frank? Hardly Wordsworth.

Frank   Fuck off, you. And County would never lose to Orient 3–2, you know nothing.

Joyce   He's right, Mr Lamb, the fashion buyers, agents, they're not giving us –

Lamb   I know, I know, look just – try and see the limitations as opportunities. To do things differently, in a, a make-do-and-mend sort of way, spirit of the Blitz. I'm saying I'm not going to be over your shoulder, you have your responsibilities, go for it.

More into the open newsroom/ compositors' room now . . .

Beverley (*arriving, with* **Diana** *in tow*)   Mr Lamb, this lady here to see you, something about horoscopes?

Lamb   Ah yes, hello you're –

Diana   Diana.

Ray   Horoscopes, that fucking voodoo nonsense, Jesus.

Diana   It isn't nonsense. It's astrology, which is a science.

Lamb   I asked you to write me a Pisces one, for yesterday?

Diana (*offering a sheet*)   Do I have the job?

Lamb   I'll tell you when you give it to me. (*He takes it and folds it into his pocket.*)

Diana   You're not gonna read it?

Lamb   No, someone else is. You'll get a call either way. (*Trying to leave.*)

Ray *with* **Frank**.

Frank   Brave new world, eh.

Ray   Yeah, don't you believe it, Larry giving free rein to anyone? Know how he got that scar on his forehead? Head-butted a stone hand so hard for not allowing a late correction it cracked both their skulls.

Frank   Fuck off.

Ray   'S what I heard.

Lamb (*pulling* **Joyce** *aside*)   And Joyce . . . I was chatting to my daughter last night. And, well, the types of models. Supermodels, most papers . . . she says a lot of girls can't relate to them, that's all. So I was wondering –

Joyce   What? That an ugly newspaper should have ugly models?

Lamb   No, I'm saying *normal* girls. Girls next door. Why don't we turn *them* into stars, eh? Like I say, though – your department, your call.

Joyce *goes*.

Lamb (*to a* **Messenger Boy**)   Here, take this logo drawing to the art department, get them to work something up –

Chapel Father (*passing*)   Oy, oy, OY! . . . Sorry, Mr Lamb, but he's not a member of the NGA, they carry drawings, that's someone's job.

Lamb (*aware this is public.*) Alright. Are you NGA?

Chapel Father   No, I'm SOGAT. Printers. Graphical and Allied Trades.

Lamb   I thought Printers were NATSOPA?

Chapel Father   Where *you* been? NATSOPA merged with NUPBPW – printing, bookbinding and paper works.

Lamb   Well can you find someone to take this from here, up to there, please?

(*As everyone goes back to work – more privately.*) Oy . . . I'm not like other editors, I came up through the unions and I want to work *with* you. But don't raise your voice to me in my own newsroom again or I swear to God – (*Beat.*) Look, we're not just making a paper *with* you, here, we want to make a paper *for* you. You and your members, all of us, right?

Chapel Father (*sarcastic*)   Aww. Thank you . . .

He goes. **Lamb** *feels the sting of that..*

Fleet Street tailors.

Murdoch *is being fitted up for a new suit. Mirrors, a tailor,* **Lamb**.

Lamb   They're not budging on the presses; unions saying it's a week's-long job to reconfigure the machines for a tabloid.

Murdoch   Bollocks, it's a three-minute job, did it myself in Adelaide. You just need to use the crushers.

Lamb   The what – ?

Murdoch   The bloody crushers. Call yourself a newsman? The crushers can fold the blasted paper over at the feed; no need to reconfigure anything. Done, easy peasy. I'll climb on to the presses when they've all gone home and do it myself, blame it on the bloody ghost if you have to – Oh, we have a ghost, by the way? Apparently.

Lamb   We do not have a ghost.

Murdoch   You don't believe in anything you can't get ink on your fingers from, do you Larry?

Lamb   Speaking of which. (*Handing him.*) From 'Diana', our potential horoscopes writer, the homework I set her.

Murdoch   Diana who?

Lamb   Dunno, she just calls herself Diana, it . . . it's in vogue. You know. 'Twiggy'. 'Jesus'. Your stars from yesterday. Accurate?

Murdoch (*reads, then pops it into his pocket*)   Yeah, good enough. (*Looking at himself in the mirror.*) Nowhere else in the world are the employees more powerful than the buggers paying 'em. They talk about solidarity, what about 'equality'? They run just as much of a closed shop as the private schools and members' clubs. Only get a job if you're the 'son to', or 'nephew of'. No wonder it's still hot metal here, bloody industrial revolution still. We have computers in Oz, *computers*!

Lamb   Got to keep them on side, work *with* folk, not *against*. Unions can refuse to print a story if they don't like it.

Murdoch (*looking at him through the reflection*)   If they do . . . I will end them.

Lamb   And when you talk about 'them' you're talking about me. If it weren't for my first union, the weekly newsletter, I wouldn't be here now. My 'people', remember?

Murdoch   Have you forgotten you're the boss now? You don't have to 'convince' anyone of anything, just bloody tell 'em, if they put up a fight, fire them.

Lamb   I just gave a speech about empowering my team, giving 'em autonomy.

Murdoch   Good, let 'em think that, but still lead them. You gotta be a pneumatic drill, Larry, never letting up, powering on through. Try it. What?

Lamb   The limited number of hacks we have don't have the manpower to go out investigating, half of them are from the regions and haven't got any bloody sources here. We still need scoops, and for that you need specialist reporters. The other papers, *their* specialists have ring-fenced the access, closed off the relationships –

Murdoch   Well then, just steal it from them.

Lamb   Steal it from them? Brilliant, OK. (*Beginning to pace around now, angrier.*) Yes, of course, as well as convincing my staff to work in disgusting conditions, with no time, or money, and become the *laughing* stock of their peers, I'll get them to become *thieves* as well, shall I?! Excellent idea!

Murdoch (*to the tailor*)   That's enough, Serge, thank you.

Tailor exits.

Murdoch   What's the matter, Larry?

Lamb   The matt— I am *trying* to fulfil the task you have entrusted to me, despite not having the necessary resources to get it bloody done! And there are still . . . 'ways of doing things', that *don't* extend to breaking journalistic codes and traditions, and becoming ever more the black sheep of the entire –

Murdoch   You're still trying to beat them by fighting on their terms. Let it go! Do you know what I hear when I hear 'codes', and 'traditions', I hear the rules as written by those who benefit from them, to stop others from treading on their turf.

He begins to remove the threads of his new suit and get changed.

I meant it when I said I wanted a bit of business acumen pumped into this Street. The markets. Competition.

It's happening everywhere else after all, can't you – feel it? The whatever-you-want-to-call-it, that 'collectivism', from your treasured unions, born out of the war, everyone together, to rebuild. Well, it's been rebuilt now. And young people today, they want to be themselves, as individuals.

This Street won't ever move forward while we think of it as a Street. Rather than individual houses, competing with one another, pushing each other forward in a fight for change, progress, the next big thing.

Lamb *listens, and takes a breath. He sits, on an upturned waste bin.*

Murdoch (*doing his tie in the mirror*)   You know, my great-grandfather, James, he was a minister, in Scotland. Split the entire Scottish church, in the 'Great Disruption' of the 1840s – isn't that wonderful, 'the great disruption'? It was too closely tied to the English Establishment, so he introduced a bit of 'competition', formed the Free Church. Heresy, yes, but there you go. I want us to *disrupt* this Street, Larry. A disruption. It's *time*.

Lamb   . . . Just steal their stuff?

Murdoch   Steal anything. Fuck it, get the readers to become the storytellers. Call in with the news, their own lives, let them bring it to us rather than us chasing them.

Lamb   You mean like . . . members of the public?

Murdoch   Why not? Normal people. Mutton – dressed as Lamb.

Isn't that the real endpoint of the revolution? When they're producing their own content themselves? That's when we know they're really getting what they want.

Lamb (*beat, sighs*)   Mutton . . . dressed as Lamb?

Murdoch (*finally back in his full – impressive – suit, arms out*) You got it.

Inside the editor's office, **Lamb***'s core team.* **Brian** *writes on two whiteboards; on one side, the* Mirror*'s features, on the other side, a blank page for the* Sun . . .

Lamb   So the *Mirror* has 'Live Letters', right, very popular, let's introduce a letters page too, and not bury it, bring it forward. What do we call it?

Joyce   Theirs is 'Live Letters'? Why don't we just call ours 'Liveliest Letters'?

Lamb   . . . Yeah, why don't we? OK, good, next.

Brian   Comic strips, obviously, the *Mirror* has Garth. A time-travelling hero.

Lamb   Alright, we'll make a time-travelling . . .

Joyce   Heroine?

Lamb   . . . Heroine, exactly. What's the *Mirror* one called, Garth? Alright Barth, Larth, Carth, Scarth – Scarth? Scarth?

Frank   Is this definitely legal?

Lamb   Dunno, next.

Brian   Their other comic, Andy Capp.

Bernard   Andy Wack, then?

Lamb   Fine.

Bernard   I was joking.

Lamb   Alright, one more step removed, *Tommy* Wack. He . . . he's a southern – fuck the cloth cap – a southern, Essex –

Brian   – beer-drinking –

Ray   – womanising –

Bernard   – van driver.

Lamb   Van driver!

Bernard   They're going to go absolutely spare over there, Larry, this is outrageous –

Lamb   It's not outrageous, these are all features, items that *we* built, remember, when we were there, when it used to be exciting, and they're wasting 'em, burying them amongst the preachy claptrap. We have a *duty* to take them back, right?

Brian   How much of that do you believe?

Lamb   All of it. What political lead is Cudlipp running week of our launch?

Beverley   Interview with Ted Heath, apparently.

Frank   I always think of the band leader, Ted Heath. That musician.

Lamb (*quick beat*)   Right, get *him* instead, exclusive.

Brian   With the band leader?

Lamb   Do it – it'll be funny, *Mirror* runs a boring old puff piece with a boring old Tory, we have a musical legend with the same name, what does *he* think about the state of the country, get to it. And finally . . . (*Writing on the board.*) I want this to be our slogan.

Frank   'Forward with the People'.

Lamb   Yeah, we're all about the people, we're the people's paper, go.

Ray   That's the old *Mirror*'s slogan. Word for word. Larry, we –

Lamb   *Old* slogan, exactly, not using it any more are they?

Bernard (*hands on his face*)   They're going to run us out of town.

Lamb   Good, we could use the exercise. Next!

A photo shoot / audition, at the Sun *offices.*

Stephanie *preparing to model some lingerie with another model,* **Chrissie**.

Beverley *prepares his camera.* **Joyce** *sits on her stool watching, smoking, reading CVs.*

Joyce   Which one is Christine?

Chrissie   Chrissie, that's me.

Beverley   Uh, could you – the robe? The dressing – could you just, erm –

Joyce   Take off your gown, honey.

Chrissie   He could have just said that. (*Takes off gown.*) What are you looking for?

Joyce   We won't be printing these, dear, this is just to get you on file.

Chrissie   You mean we don't get paid.

Joyce   Expenses, for your trouble.

Beverley   Smile?

Chrissie   Hard to smile when you're working for free.

Beverley (*shooting*)   Great, and, and more to the side, with a – maybe try a little –

Joyce   Stephanie? Is that Kahn?

Stephanie (*coming forward*)   Yes.

Chrissie *swaps out with* **Stephanie**.

Joyce   Haven't I seen you before? I'm very good with faces, don't you sing down the club?

Stephanie   I've got a lot of jobs, I'm paying for my studies.

Joyce   What are you studying?

Stephanie   It's a drama school.

Joyce   Oh, an actress, really?

Beverley (*stopping shooting* **Chrissie**)   Thank you.

Joyce   And 'Kahn', is that your stage name?

Stephanie   My father was Indian.

Joyce   Was? Did he change?

Stephanie   No, he passed away. Last year.

Joyce   Oh.

Beverley   Like Shere Khan, *Jungle Book*.

Joyce   I can see you've got a 'bit' of colour, not a huge amount. How's the course going, dear?

Stephanie   Fine, thank you. Doing *Tamburlaine* at the moment, 's alright I s'pose. I prefer comedy.

Joyce   Comedy, really. A comedy model, Beverley, what do we make of that?

Chrissie   Her name's Stephanie, not Beverley.

Beverley   No, she was – talking to me. Nice big smile then, come on.

Stephanie   What's the story I'm playing?

Joyce   There is no story, we just need your photo on file, love. This Kahn name, are you very attached to it?

Stephanie   Well it's very attached to me, yes.

Joyce   I'm just looking out for you, dear, because you are much lighter than the name suggests and I'm thinking there might be more work available to you than that. What about something more European, but still a little exotic, something like . . .

I'm just thinking.

Beverley   Rahn? There's a German footballer I know called Rahn.

Joyce   Rahn I like. Have you ever thought of maybe some blonde streaks as well, in your hair, maybe?

Stephanie   German? Blonde hair? What is this, Hitler Youth?

Beverley   That's you done.

Joyce   It's just a bit of advice, dear, you can take it or leave it, but regardless it's never a wise tactic to get lippy with the lady who decides who gets the work.

Stephanie   . . . Sorry, Mrs Hopkirk.

Joyce   That's alright, Ms . . . ?

Stephanie   . . . Rahn. Stephanie Rahn.

The old Press Club.

Hugh Cudlipp *having dinner with* **Sir Percy**, *a* Mirror *board member.*

Cudlipp *has his trademark glass of champagne on the go.*

Lamb *watches them for a while before sitting at the booth / table behind / next to them.*

Lamb (*to a waiter*)   Scotch on the rocks, please.

Cudlipp (*hearing, turning*)   Well, well. Percy, you remember Mr Lamb, used to be on the bench as a sub? He's about to try his hand at our old *Sun*.

Percy   Oh! Goodness me, you're Mr Lamb? Well . . .

Cudlipp   Percy Roberts is our new managing director of the Mirror Group. He's been overseeing our West African and Caribbean papers.

Percy   Hugh is making me sound more exotic, I've mainly been overseeing the northern distribution of the *Mirror*. Don't Forget the North, that's my tip.

A **Delivery Boy** *arrives with some proofs for* **Cudlipp**.

Delivery Boy   Mr Cudlipp?

Percy   Well, I'll leave you to look at tomorrow's edition. (*At* **Lamb**.) Pleasure.

Percy *goes. A different* **Delivery Guy** *arrives at* **Lamb***'s table with likewise some oversized sheets of paper.*

Delivery Guy   Mr Lamb.

Lamb   Thank you.

Cudlipp *smiles, getting the game.*

Cudlipp   Look at you, Larry. Taking dinner at the club, delivery of the mock-ups. You're not even going to print for a week, can't imagine what you're pretending to look at.

Lamb   Just some ideas, designs, you know.

Cudlipp   Hmm. *Liveliest* Letters, perhaps? Or *Scarth*?

Lamb   Sounds like someone has been slipping you our post, Hugh.

Cudlipp   I knew *he'd* go low. But *you*? Everyone liked you, Larry. I didn't promote you to editor, and now you're seeing red. Quite – literally.

Lamb   It was just the nearest coloured pen I had to hand, Hugh, pure coincidence. That's genuinely true.

Cudlipp   We've spoken to our lawyers –

Lamb   We've spoken to ours, you don't own 'red', Hugh.

Cudlipp   It's – a great responsibility. Having the ear of the working classes –

Lamb   Oh Hugh, it's bloody chip-wrapping, end of the day, / 'responsibility' –

Cudlipp   *Yours* maybe – yes, you can scoff, but I've – we've worked hard to change things here, why? Because I happen to care about the bettering of people's lives, from the place I come from, *you* come from. To politically enable the next you, or me, all of us, with tools to forge our own collective destiny. / Is that such a –

Lamb   Sorry, our destiny, or your version of it? What about – yes collective, fine, but what about / individual people with, individual –

Cudlipp   What, you have a problem with that term now? After only a few weeks in your paymaster's company. They called you 'Red Larry' way back when, if I recall –

Lamb   Oh, have you not seen the colour of our logo? Still flying the flag.

Cudlipp   . . . Do you think, genuine question –

Waiter   Sir. (*Delivering the bill.*)

Cudlipp   Thank you – that it is a coincidence the average man's lot has significantly improved, this past decade? That these steps forward would have happened without a, yes, popular but pioneering paper placing pressure on the government? And you, what great contribution will you be offering the national conversation, now that you're finally – all those years, Larry! – finally at the helm?

Lamb   . . . We'll be – we're gonna to be doing a lot of 'human stories'.

Cudlipp   'Human stories'. Ah.

Lamb   I mean we're – God you've always been so squeamish about just natural human desires, haven't you? There's something about basic needs that makes you a bit – (*Mock shivers.*) Yurk. Doesn't it? That's what I mean about individual . . . I don't know, 'self-expression', of young people who – yeah, who maybe *don't* want the grey uniformity of, of Hugh Cudlipp's working class, where *this* is the club and you *must* pay your subs and *this* is good for you, *this* is bad, read this, / listen to that –

Cudlipp   Oh so only *Guardian* readers, or *The Times* should have the Chancellor's Budget explained to them? / Only the *Telegraph* should –

Lamb   I've no problem with the Budget, Hugh, we'll be reporting on the Budget, it's how / you do it –

Cudlipp   – should be introduced to classical music? You know I remember . . . how much I hated school, God I hated it. So boring. I'd leave as soon as that bell went, but one day, I recall, these musicians came in, two violinists, one cello and a . . . (*Thinks.*) A viola! Yes. Some scheme I imagine, funded by some workers' educational programme, and for whatever reason, I stayed. And they played this piece of . . . (*Sighs.*) Schubert. And Larry. It changed me. Hah-hah-hah, yes I know, but it changed me. I *ran*. I went home like the fucking wind, I don't know why, and when I got home, that night, I couldn't even speak. They called the doctor! Thought I had a fever, I'm not even joking. If someone had denied to me that 'beauty' . . .

(*Beat. Checks his watch.*) You could come with me, now, I'm off to Wigmore Hall, second half of St Matthew Passion. For old times.

Lamb   . . . Do you really sit there listening to all that, Hugh, or do you just feel like you should?

Cudlipp   Oh, bugger off. Singing is the weapon of the Welsh working classes.

Lamb   There is actually a thing called pop music, now, it's been all the rage, for like, a decade, it's actually quite good. Stands for 'popular' – think of it like the popping of champagne corks, only it's for everyone, pop, pop, pop.

Cudlipp (*to the* **Waiter***, having put money in the bill*)   Thank you. (*Stands.*) Pander to and promote the most *base* instincts of people all you like, fine, create an appetite, but I warn you. You'll have to keep feeding it.

He goes. **Lamb** *momentarily sits alone for a moment, festering on this. He might look after where* **Cudlipp** *went, about to follow, before . . .*

Lamb   Ah, fuck it –

He exits the other way.

Editor's office – the clattering and ringing from the newsroom outside.

Senior staff **Brian**, **Bernard**, **Joyce**, **Frank**, **Ray**, **Diana**, **Beverley** *with* **Lamb**.

'4 Days to Go' on the flip chart.

Lamb *bursts around the office, fizzing with chaotic energy, tearing mock-ups off the wall.*

Lamb   Wait, stop, stop. We're – we're not there yet. Spike what we've got, I wanna start again.

A reaction from the senior team.

Brian   Wow! Boss? (*At his watch.*) There's only –

Lamb   We're not there yet, we can't just be a cheaper imitation of theirs, well what's the point? No, we have to, to be more *honest* – we're still *censoring* ourselves, What People Want, well, what do *We* Want, we're all, aren't we, from working fucking class bloody – what do *you* want, and like, and need. Don't worry what anyone thinks, why are we ashamed? Fuck it. I . . .

I Don't Like Brass Bands. There.

Bernard   Oh no, so evocative, makes the / hairs on my arms –

Lamb   I know I should, my . . . dad, in a colliery band, but effing Elgar and bloody Holst, it just – it's such a *downer*, and I hated having to learn an instrument –

Beverley   Aw, Mum's still got me on the clarinet.

Lamb   All them hours, just to 'better myself'? Well fuck it –

Bernard   Don't listen to him, very useful skill –

Lamb   I like, I like Ray Charles, and Charlie Parker, I like *noise*, Dave Clark on the drums – (*Imitating drums.*) Bababadadabdamdum!

Joyce   And that's drums, is it?

Lamb (*writing on the board*)   'Who are we?' *Really*. What excites you, tickles you? I mean it, say things, anything. Bernard?

Bernard   I don't – you mean like, hobbies, or – ?

Lamb   Anything! In your spare time!

Bernard   . . . No, you'll think it's weird.

Diana   Aw, we won't, tell us.

Bernard   Well, I, I . . . I quite enjoy adapting the lesser-known works of Emile Zola from French into English.

Lamb   . . . O–OK . . . (*Goes to write it down, can't be bothered.*) Anyone else? Brian?

Brian   I like producing a newspaper on time and on –

Lamb   We *are* doing, come on.

Brian (*shrugs*)   . . . Smoking and drinking.

Lamb (*writing*)   Right. Good. Me too.

Brian   Can't make a paper on smoking and drinking.

Lamb   Why not, if it's what people do? Frank, you, likes, loves?

Frank   Well… you know, sport, obviously. Love it.

Lamb   Sports, yes, but which sports, the sports papers cover?

Frank   Well, you know, football obviously, cricket and . . . you know, fishing.

Lamb   Fishing. Yep. But . . . really? You really like fishing?

Frank   Well . . . (*Feeling the eyes of the room.*) No, actually I can't stand it, it's boring.

Lamb   Right, yes, so –

Frank   It's *really* boring! I only did it 'cause of me dad –

Lamb   So fuck your dad! – Oh, sorry, I don't mean that –

Frank   No *fuck* him, you're right! I like, I like *boxing*, I like fighting, organised fighting, and I don't just wanna read the scores, I wanta *see* it, pictures, the blood and the sweat and broken noses and grrrrr.

Diana   I want to talk about other people, gossip, I *love* gossip, I'm sorry, but I want to poke my nose into other people's lives, my neighbours, everyone.

Lamb   The lives of normal people, behind closed doors.

Joyce   And famous people. The Royal Family!

Lamb   Treat famous people, the Royals, like they *are* Normal People.

Frank   Wha–at, nothing normal about that lot.

Lamb   Why? Queen still has to wipe her arse, doesn't she?

Joyce   LARRY!

Lamb   More, this is good, more!

Diana   OK, OK, I like going out! Like proper out, like dancing, really *dancing*, sweaty and loud and where you drink so much you think you gonna be sick, and not fucking Babycham, I want beer! *Pints* of BEER!

Beverley   Yeah, down the Marquis Club, or the Palais! Cheeky chasers, pulling birds!

Frank   Eh, look at this dark horse here! Lady's man.

Beverley   Oh, *I* don't actually do that – Oh, I thought this was like a wish list – sorry, I get the game now. Gardening?

Joyce   Alright, telly, then.

Lamb   Television!

Diana   I like watching telly. Hours of it, not talking to anyone, not my husband, my fucking kids. Just watching the telly. Staring at it, like a zombie, for hours, it's brilliant.

Lamb   Why don't papers talk about telly?

Brian   Telly's our rival, we don't want them watching telly.

Lamb   But people *do*, because they *want* to, so let's be the first paper that says 'That's OK'. Listings, interviews, features, let's have eight – no – twelve pages!

Bernard   Of bloody *television*?!

Lamb   Yep, centre page pull-out, we'll move the international page to –

Bernard   We're not moving that, we need that.

Lamb   Is that what you're really interested in? That's what you wake up thinking about. What's going on in Washington or Moscow or Paris?

Bernard   Yes. It is. Well, obviously, you know . . . that and the weather.

Lamb   The weather.

Bernard   Yeah, I suppose . . . *(Shifts in his seat.)* I suppose I wonder . . . quite a lot . . . what the weather might be up to, that day.

Lamb   So . . . do you maybe, deep down . . . maybe want the weather to be on page two instead?

Bernard *(beat; getting into it now)*   Yeah, I want the weather on page two . . . I want it on page two!

Lamb   Yeah! And why?

Bernard   Because I'm British, and that's what I want to talk about?!

Lamb   Right!

Joyce   Famous people, rock stars, the royal family. Gossip about *them* and –

Diana   And normal people, what's really going on in their lives.

Frank   You're meant to be a clairvoyant.

Diana   Yeah, but that's looking up at the stars, I wanna peek through people's net curtains. Don't look at me like that, we all do.

Beverley   Yeah, it's true. Not in that way, peeping Tom, just –

Brian   I mean, I'm just going to say it . . . free stuff. I like being given free stuff.

Frank   I fucking love free stuff.

Lamb   Free stuff.

Brian   When you beat someone, at something, anything! I like 'winning'.

Beverley   Oh, winning's brilliant. Losing is terrible, but winning –

Frank   When England win!

Ray   Or when you win in a fight!

Bernard   Or when you win at bingo! (*Small beat off their look.*) Right fuck off, because it's actually an incredibly aggressive sport, I've seen people get really hurt.

Lamb   And, it's working class! And, it's popular! Bingo!

Ray   Women! I like, I like pretty women. Legs. Their legs, and, and boobs. And bums, bums, I like bums! –

Diana   Well, if we're having women – men then, too, handsome men.

Joyce   Well, then, someone should say it. *Sex.* In fact our women's page – that brings up a conversation we had on our desk this morning, the direction of our women's page – well, much as we're happy to run the usual rubbish about recipes and clothes, well, we also want to talk about sex. Because – and I really don't want to unsettle anyone or anything but, well – women masturbate.

Silence.

Frank   No, they don't.

Joyce   Frank. Your wife. She masturbates.

Beat.

Frank   *Why?*

Joyce   Fact is, there's a difference between plastering pretty women all over your rag as a sex object, and recognising that women objectively enjoy sex.

Lamb   Of course. Women like sex. Men like sex. Which, we could reference, just for now . . . (*Writing.*) Under the umbrella term . . . as – love.

Joyce   'Love'. I would never have picked you out as a prude, Mr Lamb.

Lamb   It's suggestive, innuendo. Shakespeare was a legend at it.

Frank   You're setting the bar very high.

Brian   For you maybe, I've published books.

Joyce   Oh, leave Frank alone! He knows about books.

Frank   Thank you –

Joyce   Spends enough time in bookmakers.

They all laugh.

Frank   Alright, alright, I've had enough of these jibes, look! No, maybe I'm not a linguist used to writing fancy-smancy features yet. No maybe I don't always get my spelling, and my grammar, and some of my facts right. And no, maybe I don't always hand my copy in on time so it can make it into the actual paper . . . (*He stops.*)

Lamb   Oh, is that it? I thought that was going somewhere.

Frank   No.

Joyce (*laughing*)   Fucking hell, Frank.

Others join in laughing too.

Lamb   See, this is my point – a sense of humour. *British* sense of humour, taking the piss, it's – 'affectionate'. If we're funny, we can get away with anything. Stops it being nasty. Because, oy, we have to remember who we're doing it for. Giving normal folk the ammunition to laugh at their so-called betters. We punch up, never down. I don't want to sound moralistic –

Bernard   Morals, heaven forbid, God no –

Lamb   But that should be our . . . 'values'. If that's not too strong a word. OK?

Winning stuff. Free stuff. Love. (*Writing those words.*) Win. Free. Love. Every time, we get these three word on to the front page of our paper – you all get a bonus.

There. That's the *Sun*. Spread the word. 'Win Free Love!'

Music kicks in, as we move into –

The newsroom – '1 Day to Go'.

Almost a montage of putting the first paper together as we jump from characters to spaces.

The **Chapel Father** *leads an* **Apprentice Printer** *around the composing room, spilling tea from a mug, constantly smoking, relighting, smoking . . .*

Chapel Father   Your uncle is – ?

Apprentice   Mick, he's in the composing room at the *Mirror* but they didn't have nothing doing for me there, so he said come here –

Chapel Father   Well, we're chucking you in at the deep end – it's launch day. We're joining you into RIRMA: Revisers,

Ink and Roller-Makers and Ancillaries. I'm your chapel father, different chapels, different fathers.

Apprentice   Should I be writing this down?

Chapel Father   No –

Frank, **Joyce**, **Brian**, *all at their typewriters, punching away, tearing their copy out and marching it over to –*

Bernard's *table, with* **Larry**, *pulling together the first pages.*

Lamb   Right, front page: 'Exclusive: Racehorse dope sensation!' Interview with the trainer who's giving his horses smack.

Beverley (*arriving with a photo*)   Picture.

Bernard   Right, headline there –

Lamb   Bigger.

Brian (*phone down, coming over*)   Boss, that garage says they'll donate a car.

Lamb   Oh yeah, we're giving away a car, page 6.

Beverley   Yeah! Win – Free – Love! (*Clicks the flash into his own eyes.*) Ow, sorry.

Bernard   Main picture there, sub-headings, side panel with listings.

Brian (*on the phone*)   Boss, guess what, Ted Heath's dead.

Everyone   What? / Shit!

Brian   No, the fucking band leader.

Frank (*genuinely sad*)   Oh no . . .

Brian   Yeah, he's gone off to the swing orchestra in the sky.

Lamb   Aw, fuck.

Ray (*entering, overalls, ink*)   Er, sorry to interrupt, the type keys have arrived. Bad news. You didn't order enough of our Large Headline Font. For a start, there's only three 'E's.

Bernard   What does that mean?

Ray   Means you can't have more than three 'E's in any one page main headline. Including front page.

They turn to look at the mock-up of the front page, the horse headline.

Brian (*counting the 'E's*)   One two, three, four – shit, five, six.

Bernard   Lose exclusive?

Frank   Wow wow wow –

Beverley   Change dope to smack? 'Race Horse Smack Sensation'?

Frank   Nah that just sounds like someone's been punching a horse.

Brian   Don't have to say *race* horse, could just be horse.

Lamb   . . . One, two, three, alright, fine. Good, get it off. Brian, any other problems with Ted Heath piece?

Brian   Are there any *other* problems?

Lamb   Yeah.

Brian   Apart from him being dead?

Lamb   Yeah.

Brian   . . . No, luckily it's just that one thing.

Lamb   Turn it into an obit, page 26. (*At* **Ray**.) You, order more 'E's? And in the meantime let's just hope nothing happens to fucking Bee Gees!

Chapel Father *at a metal desk in the newsroom.* **Frank** *jots down copy,* **Chapel Father** *referencing his work.*

Chapel Father   Journalists – different union from printers, altogether, NUJ – they type their bollocks –

Frank   Bollocks bollocks, bullshit bullshit, there –

Chapel Father   Drop the page here, messenger boy brings it over to –

They go to the 'back bench' now, **Frank** *having joined the tour (a Pied Paper accumulative effect).*

The back bench is a horseshoe of desks. **Ray Mills** *the sub arrives in his position.*

Chapel Father   The back bench, the sub, takes the copy, edits it –

Ray (*scribbling*)   Nope, nope, bollocks, he doesn't play for West Ham; that's shit. 'God' should be capitalised . . .

Frank   Sorry –

Chapel Father   Then over to the composing room.

Lamb (*bumping into* **Frank**)   Frank! Your sports page leader.

Frank   Ye-ah!

Lamb (*grabbing him*)   I love it! 'Sports with Four Rows of Teeth!' Grrr.

Frank   Grrr!

Lamb   And George Best guest column?

Frank   I figure instead of doing all the work, just get them to do it instead.

Joyce (*handing in copy to* **Ray**)   Women's lead – 'Being a mother doesn't mean you have to join the cabbages'.

Ray   I can't sub that, I don't know what any of it means.

Joyce (*taking it back*)   Good, it's not for you.

She hands it straight to the **Apprentice**, *who continues with the* **Chapel Father**. **Joyce** *following now, part of the 'tour' as they come to a* **Linotype Operator** *at his machine.*

Hot molten lead, burning orange, melts down a pig into a pot by the machine – all this resembling a Tolkien-esque foundry, more than what many would think of as a modern newsroom – sweat, mess, dirt, sparks, ink.

Chapel Father   Each sentence has to be fashioned and set in hot metal, here's all your different moulds, every letter, colon, full stop. Your pot of molten metal there – Don't touch. Dave here sets the line of type.

Operator *is punching heavy keys. Smash, smash, smash – the line of type is forged out of the machine, steaming.*

Chapel Father   Same process, every single letter of every word, every line of type, in the whole entire paper, forged from scratch, every single day. This take goes into the galley here – (*A small box, which the* **Operator** *takes over to . . .*) And that all goes to the Random.

Apprentice   Why's it called the Random?

Chapel Father   I don't know, it's random.

The 'take' placed down with other takes into a full box. An **Inker** *places a sheet down, paints ink across it – he's covered in the stuff.*

Chapel Father   Ink the full type of the article with a roller on this sheet, take this sheet over to the reading room to be proofed.

Apprentice *takes the sheet to a separate area where suddenly . . . there's almost complete silence.*

A **Reader** *sits quietly, glasses on the end of his/her nose, reading the proof with the occasional huff.*

He/she nods and hands it to the **Apprentice** *who takes it back into . . . the world of clattering and smashing chaos.*

Chapel Father   Then all the takes for that page arrive here, at the 'stone'.

The stone – a free-standing heavy metal table, waist-height. A **Stone Hand** *on one hand, a* **Stone Sub** *on the other.* **Beverley** *and* **Frank** *join here now.*

Over in a part of the newsroom, **Bernard Shrimsley** *has arrived at his art desk, carefully directing his Anglepoise lamp on to his layout pad.*

Chapel Father   Stone hand, following the layout from the art editor, arranges the page into this chase. Stone sub that side still has time to make corrections. Stone sub can never step on *this* side of the stone, stone hand can never step on *that* side. We don't want a repeat of the troubles of '64, do we?

Beverley / Frank / Joyce (*laughing, clueless*)   No / course not.

Chapel Father   When everyone's happy –

The **Stone Hand** *raises a large mallet into the air – and strikes, hard, down on the metal plates. Heavy, hard, brutal, sweating, again and again, as ink occasionally hits his apron, the odd spark.*

Chapel Father   Then, we make a flong from resin, which is sent to the foundry to be cast as a plate –

A flash from the foundry, a curved metal plate hangs down –

– which is then sent down to the machine room, to be fixed to the presses.

Everyone has headed back to their respective stations, leaving **Chapel Father** *and* **Apprentice**.

Apprentice   So . . . what should I be doing then?

Chapel Father (*handing him his mug*)   Make us another, will yer?

Back at **Bernard**'s *desk, with* **Lamb** *and* **Brian**.

Lamb   Double spread here with the Rolling Stones at their Hollywood mansion – use that one with the girl in it, not that one, and go. (*At his watch, then passing* **Brian** *and* **Bernard**.) Bri, make sure everything looks shipshape on deck. The 'captain's' about to come aboard . . .

Brian   The man himself? So he *is* real after all . . .

Murdoch *appears, possibly through the smoke and hiss of the foundry, into –*

Lamb's *office.*

Murdoch *is waiting with* **Anna Murdoch***.*

Murdoch   So? What have you got for me?

Anna   Larry, how are you?

Murdoch   You remember Anna.

Lamb   Yes of course. (*Kisses on the cheek.*) Look, slight spanner in the works, you pushing the button to set the presses rolling on the first –

Murdoch   She's pushing the bloody button, Larry! It'll make a great picture, where's that kid with the camera?

Lamb   Unions won't let her push the button unless she becomes a member of NATSOPA, which / is . . . but I've –

Murdoch   Bullshit, which bastards – bring 'em here.

Anna   Rupert, let Larry talk.

Lamb   But I've squared it, you can just become an honorary, temporary member, alright, just to make us all square.

Murdoch   I'm not having my wife – this is my paper, I'm / paying for –

Anna   It's alright. Honestly, I've no . . . It sounds fun, being a signed-up member of the team, even if only temporary. What do I do?

Lamb   Bri?!

Brian *comes in.*

Lamb   He'll take you to the − thing.

Anna *gives* **Rupert** *a 'don't worry' kiss, leaving.*

Lamb   Are you ready?

Murdoch   I was about to ask you the same thing.

Lamb   To make a speech to the team.

Murdoch   Oh Christ, can't you just do that, I hate being −

Lamb   They should know who you are, you're too . . . They find you 'remote'.

Murdoch   They should be grateful I'm 'remote'.

Lamb   You could talk to them, ask them questions, talk about yourself, like a normal person.

Murdoch   Can't stand 'chit chat', especially about myself. They'll get used to it.

Sir Alick *and* **Muriel McKay** *enter.*

Sir Alick   Whey! All set for the off.

Murdoch   Muriel. A vision as always, what are you still doing with this chump?

Muriel   I just saw Anna, you're setting her up on the factory floor I hear. Making her sing for her supper.

Sir Alick *(at his watch)*   Come on, tick-tock, tick-tock.

Muriel   One second. *(With a make-up compact.)* Larry, you don't mind?

Sir Alick *and* **Murdoch** *exit into the main floor.* **Lamb** *putting on a tie,* **Muriel** *doing her make-up in the mirror.*

Muriel   It'll be fine, you know.

Lamb   Better be more than fine, fucking hell. Sorry.

Muriel   For what, swearing? Oh no, how will I ever fucking cope? (*Finishes powdering.*) You're feeling the pressure, I get it, course.

Lamb   . . . 'S just, you only get one chance to launch your – to *prove* your . . . and, we're trying to do something, here, that if it doesn't – then . . .

I mean it's fine, maybe, if you oversee several bloody papers, but when this is your only . . . when it's *yours*, and . . . ah, shut up, Larry, rambling.

Muriel   No, I know. You shouldn't think this doesn't matter to them, you know. Especially Rupert. I know he comes across all 'roll of the dice, who cares', but when he goes for something. He goes all in. He's all in on this one, Larry. We all are.

She touches his arm, and goes. After a moment, **Lamb** *follows.*

Stephanie Rahn *arrives into the busy newsroom, bumping into Bernard –*

Stephanie   Excuse me sorry, I'm looking for –

Bernard (*passing, briskly*)   We're all looking for something, love.

He goes. **Brian** *passes.*

Stephanie   Hello? Where's Mrs Hopkirk?

Brian   Really not the day to be looking for working, dear –

Stephanie   I've done the work, I want to get paid please.

Brian   Cashier's department, downstairs. (*Looks.*) I know you. Page 17.

Stephanie   I don't know what page they put me on.

Brian   You're part of the team then now – no escape. Wanna see your face come off the presses, several hundred thousand times? . . . Come.

They head to the machine room.

Everyone gathers together as through the staff steps –

Rupert Murdoch. *Flanked by* **Anna** *and* **Lamb**.

Murdoch   Well, I'm . . . not one for big – you know.
Speeches. In front of . . . I just felt beholden to say a – well.

A few weeks ago . . . I asked this man here, Larry Lamb . . .
to consider the impossible. To take something old, and make it
new. And so he's taken a lot that is borrowed, yes, and made
something a bit – 'blue'.

Some laughter.

But, seriously . . . I think – that this matters. What we're doing.
You've decided . . . to 'give people what they want'. Something
so radical – and yet so simple. To hold up a mirror – pardon
the pun . . . to ourselves. And to hell with the consequences
if we don't like what we see. It's who we are. This year, they
landed a rocket on the moon. Tomorrow, we give the world a
new *Sun*. That will spread its light, into every dark corner of
the Establishment. Of the powerful. Of the corrupt. And yes,
of 'normal people', as well, if that happens to be a story
normal people want to read. The noise we begin making now,
in this basement, may well just echo around the world.

Anna, my darling wife.

Anna Murdoch *pushes a button. A groaning newsroom – the lights
cut out.*

From the darkness . . .

Murdoch   Shit.

Later. **Lamb**'s *office.* **Lamb** *pours himself a whisky. Checks the time.*

In the print room, **Bench Hands** *toss bundles of newspapers to one
another, through the air . . .*

Around Fleet Street – the different newspaper editors open the edition, the names of their own newspapers lit up. The Guardian, The Times, *the* Express . . .

The Sun *editor's office.* **Murdoch** *steps in.*

Murdoch   Well, editor? What's the news?

Lamb (*drinks*)   News is . . . the two-hour delay to get the presses running again, means we missed most of the last trains north. The paper itself . . . well, I think the one record we may have broken is the most spelling mistakes and errors in any one paper in the history of the Street. And that every other editor right now will be jumping for joy. I'm sorry. We can do better, we will –

Murdoch   You worked miracles, Larry. It shouldn't have been possible.

Sir Alick (*arriving with champagne, glasses*)   Knock, knock. Here we go.

Murdoch   I don't think Larry's in the mood, Alick.

Sir Alick   Oh come on, as the deputy chairman, handing out booze is my only responsibility, don't take that away from me?

Murdoch (*with the paper*)   I think it looks alright? There's a – a 'charm' to it. Just as I asked. Rough, and . . . almost ready.

Lamb   What's the word on the Street? What are they saying?

Sir Alick   The *Mirror* are throwing a, erm . . . a 'Sigh of Relief' party. A message, saying they're not worried in the slightest.

Murdoch   They won't be as smug when our sales come in.

Lamb   With half the country missing? Don't hold your breath.

Sir Alick   Something came for you.

He points. A large box. **Lamb** *opens it. Beat. He removes –*

– a dying sunflower, in a pot.

Lamb (*reading the note*)   'A spare centrepiece, from our party tonight. Thought you might like one of your own . . . '

Beat. He punches a small mirror on the wall, it cracks a little. A moment.

Right.

He starts writing his own note.

The Mirror *newsroom.*

Mirror *reporters are gathered, a party in full swing. Dying sunflowers in pots, placed around.*

Lee   Ladies and gents, your chairman and leader, Hugh Cudlipp!

Cheers.

Cudlipp   Well, though we await the *Sun*'s first figures this evening, I am pleased to report that as our little ears on the ground suggested to us, long in advance – their shit sheet does, in fact, really stink. (*Some laughter.*) And we can be proud, and must remain proud, that we held our nerve, and did not lose our dignity, to compete with an enemy who in fact does not exist.

To the *Mirror*, and to all of you! Resolve!

All   Resolve!

Cudlipp *and co. retire to –*

The Mirror *editor's office,* **Cudlipp**, **Lee** *and* **Percy**.

Cudlipp   Go on. Are they out?

In the Sun *editor's office, opposite . . .* **Lamb**, **Murdoch** *and* **Sir Alick**.

The phone rings. **Sir Alick** *takes it.*

Sir Alick   Yes? . . . Yes, go for it. (*Writing, pencil, pad.*) Ah-uh. And that's London is it? The north?

And Wales. And then . . . ? Right-o. Thank you. (*Phone down.*)

Murdoch   Just say it, don't fucking sugar-coat it.

Sir Alick *is adding up.*

Lamb   It went down? Just at least say we didn't go down, please, fuck.

Sir Alick *finally tots it up. He takes his glasses off and moves to* **Lamb**, *gesturing for* **Murdoch**.

Sir Alick   Here, come here.

He puts his arm around both their shoulders . . .

In the Mirror.

Lee (*with the figures*)   They broke a million. About a million and one.

Cudlipp   And ours, today?

Lee   Four point . . . six. So, you know, we're way ahead, barely a dent but –

Cudlipp   But there has been a dent. It came from us. They left us, to go there?

Percy (*entering*)   Sorry to disturb. I was told this was urgent.

She hands **Cudlipp** *a large item wrapped in brown paper.*

Cudlipp *rips the brown paper off his delivery.*

He reveals the mirror, cracked, from **Lamb**'s *office.*

He almost smiles. Hanging it up, possibly . . . They all stare at it for a moment . . .

If they want this to be personal . . .

Percy   Hugh, it isn't personal, it's intimidation. David throwing stones at Goliath. They quite literally *cannot* get close to us. One million compared to nearly five?

Cudlipp   You bloody fools, can't you see what this is? David and Goliath? Percy, do you not know how it ends in your own fucking metaphor! We're standing in Rome, gentlemen! And you know how Rome fell? An invasion of the barbarian hordes! Sodomy and sin. Well you might think girls and crime and celebrities and *bonking*, are harmless but it's the first crack in the dam, I swear.

We're moving between both Sun *and* Mirror *now.*

Murdoch   . . . *Yes.* I knew it. We knew it, Larry! COME ON!

Lamb   (*sitting now, taking a breath*)   They bought it. People wanted to buy it . . .

Murdoch   And this when we're only at half-cock, imagine when we're going at full fucking pelt! When we're all cylinders firing.

(*Running to Lamb, grabbing him.*) That's my boy. That's my BOY! Fuck! Fuck yes, YES!

Lee   Look, maybe there's *something* in it. In this – 'fun'.

Lamb   Shit, we're actually going to take them on, aren't we?

Murdoch   Oh 'take them on'? Fuck that. I want to *destroy* them. I want to crush them all, grind them down into the dirt! We *can* –

Lamb   OK, alright, yes, we did good, but, a step at a time –

Murdoch   No, no, Larry, look at me. We're right, we're being proven right. (*In the direction of the* Mirror.) The past (*At them.*) The future. Past. Future.

Cudlipp   You might think it's all harmless? Celebrities, and bonking? Don't you know how Rome fell?

Murdoch   One year!

Cudlipp   An invasion of the barbarian hordes!

Lamb   What's one year?

Murdoch   My challenge, to you, to beat the *Mirror*.

Cudlipp   Sodomy, and sin!

Murdoch   A year today, the anniversary of our launch. (*Laughing.*) Wouldn't that just be the most fucking incredible –?

Sir Alick   It's the largest selling paper in the world –

Murdoch   Exactly! What a story that would be. What *proof*, that we're –

Lamb   That would . . . to even come close to that would – (*At* **Cudlipp**.) – end him.

Murdoch   So?! (*Holding up the sunflower.*) Look how they laughed, they *laughed* at you, Larry. From inside their exclusive little clubs!

Percy   Let's not lose perspective –

Cudlipp   Goddammit this is a war!

Murdoch   We can do this, Larry. You and I, together. Fuck the Street. They're old, we're new. They're wrong, we're right. Let's burn it all down, and start again.

Cudlipp   And if it's war they want, by God, they'll get it.

Murdoch   . . . Larry?

Lamb *comes forward, and lights a cigarette. Inhales. And nods.*

Lamb   . . . There'll be a lot of blood.

Murdoch   God, I hope so.

Act Two

A TV camera monitor flickers on . . .

A black-and-white close-up on **Murdoch***'s face, sitting in a chair in a TV studio. Prepping for an interview, checking his hair, a sip of water. Occasionally looking down the lens towards us . . .*

Snippets of distorted sound, which we may recognise from the future – the football stadium chants of a football game 'L – I – V –E – R – P . . . ', the launch of the Falklands Armada to 'Land of Hope and Glory', the dialling in of a teenage girl's voicemail, testimony to a Parliamentary Committee, 'the most humble day of my life . . . ', the aggressive, shouty tones of Fox News anchors – and, possibly, incongruously for now, the growing sound of pigs snuffling around in dirt . . .

The lights snap on. TV studio at London Weekend Television.

Murdoch   Now look, I don't pretend that we're –

Host   But the accusations, Mr Murdoch, not just accusations, the personal feelings of many people, including myself, when I'm – I have to say 'forced' to spend many dismal hours reading your paper, in order / to prepare for –

Murdoch   It doesn't bother me what you think, or other people in the London media, it bothers me what normal people in the rest of the country think, and it's normal people who are buying it –

Host   Well, yes, if you will wallow in material that is sleazy, and downmarket –

Murdoch   I don't agree that it's sleazy, I think it's fun, and I don't like this term downmarket. Who is the arbiter of whether or not something is up, or down. You?

Host   Well no, not just me actually, the Press Council has made a formal complaint about your paper, leading figures from the Church as you know – we played the Cardinal earlier. Even the royal family have expressed their concerns, you

having personally made an enemy of His Royal Highness
Prince Philip.

Murdoch (*chuckles*)   Yes, I . . . (*Beat, more serious.*) Yes.

Host   Explain to me then, the positive merits of *this* double-
page spread. The Rolling Stones in their Hollywood mansion.
with scantily clad or naked –

Murdoch   The *suggestion* of nudity, never seen –

Host   – girls, drinking, taking drugs, lounging about with all
of their money?

Murdoch   The positive merits are that people *bought* it. In
soaring numbers.

Host   And that's it, is it?

Murdoch   I'm not going to sugar-coat it, I shouldn't have to.
Every editor knows it, but if I have to be the first one that says
it – fine, yes, the numbers are what matter.

Host   So the news business then, for generations seen as a
noble pursuit, engendering public debate, seen as exactly that
by your own father –

Murdoch   My . . . Let me tell you about my father –

Host   You, on the other hand, his *son*, see the primary
function of the *Sun* as no different from that of hawking soap,
or shaving cream on a market stall, it's solely about shifting
volume.

Murdoch   Listen . . .

When a political party increases its vote share, that's seen as an
indication of democratic intent and you place them into
government. So why then is circulation not just as good a
measure of the will of the people? *Better*, in fact, because the
choice at the ballot box is a false choice. Two options, this or
that. Whereas the marketplace . . . supply and demand, what
you are willing to part with your pennies for – *that's* pure
democracy. Modern democracy. Real choice.

Host   But beyond that, because what graces the pages of our newspapers – or do you disagree? – is about our own national narratives, the stories we tell ourselves, *about* ourselves, and what you're saying, as we enter this new decade, a fresh start, is –

Murdoch   What I'm saying is that countries reinvent themselves all the time, and –

Host   And in reinventing England, then, Great Britain, in *your* own image – what will we be? Because judging by this, we are ruder, and coarser –

Murdoch   Less reverential, I would say, and less in awe of – and I have to say actually, that any controversy, which I don't happen to recognise, is being whipped up by a sort of Establishment who for so long –

Host   Ah, now, you come back to this again and again, Mr Murdoch, and I have to say that is an Australian view of England – it really is, because it doesn't work that way any more. I mean of course, still, with the daft old-school ties and so on, but it's not an organised 'conspiracy' against people.

Murdoch   You reckon?

Host   Are you not part of this Establishment now? Seen being driven around town in your Rolls-Royce –

Murdoch   Oh, so you're talking about material things, well –

Host   Well you, in the *Sun*, often talk of little else, free giveaways, what to buy, what to wear –

Murdoch   It's absolutely OK to want things, in my view, even though I actually have very little desire for lots of things myself, or for being the centre of attention –

Host   And yet you're here. On television . . .

Moving into . . .

The editor's office of the Sun.

Larry Lamb *sits, feet up, whisky on the go, watching* **Murdoch** *on the television.*

Host   Look – the cameras, they're pointing at you. The other chairmen, owners, they're behind their desks. Why are you here?

Murdoch   We want to reach people.

Music kicks in…

The Sun *team arrive.* **Brian, Joyce, Ray, Beverley, Bernard, Diana** *and more strutting down the Street, and tossing copies of the* Sun *out to the audience and into the crowd, raucous and celebratory, and defiant.*

Various punning headlines comic and vulgar appearing around them . . .

The Sun, *editor's office.*

Brian *at the whiteboard.*

Brian   So, we've had 'puppy week', 'parrot week', 'cake week', 'beer week', 'ooh-lah-lah' week, we're running out of giveaways.

Frank   Pussy week?

Joyce (*whacking him*)   Frank.

Frank   As in cats! Kittens!

Joyce   The trading standards lot will be having kittens if you launch something called pussy week, I tell you.

Lamb   Sounds good to me – go for it. We've confirmed the serialisation rights for this smutty book, *The Sensuous Woman*?

Joyce   It isn't smut, it's a helpful guide for everything in the bedroom you're too afraid to ask.

Diana   I couldn't get through a single page without going red.

Beverley   I'll take it off you, if it's –

Bernard   We're going hard on Friday with a promotion on the masthead next week – 'The *Sun*, now only 5p'.

Ray   Wait, weren't it 5p last week?

Bernard   Yes. And now it's *still* only 5p – right, Mr Lamb?

Lamb   We're low on real-life crime serials, anything coming out of the courts?

Brian   We have the 'Exmouth Ex with an Axe' murder tomorrow, but –

Lamb   The readers go potty for ones that combine sex *and* violence, blood and lust, that's the sweet spot. Dig deep, bury your head in the filth, sniff out something juicy for the morning of the *Mirror*'s magazine launch.

Bernard   Ramadan starts this week, boss, shouldn't we, I dunno, maybe find a, a 'fun' way in to that.

Brian   They can't kiss for a month, I know that much.

Lamb   They can't kiss through Ramadan? Alright, get Kate and Geoff to whip up something cheeky on 'no kissing after midnight for half a million Muslims', keep it light.

As the others leave, when –

Diana, do us a favour? Tomorrow's scopes. Make 'his' – optimistic, would you? Confident, I don't want him to be having any . . . wobbles. When he wobbles he –

Diana   Are you suggesting I manipulate the reading of every Pisces in the land, just so you can manipulate the mood of Mr Murdoch?

Lamb   Yeah, why not, it's all bollocks anyway, may as well be useful bollocks.

Diana   I was kidding. Course I will, although don't call it bollocks.

Lamb   . . . Do you . . . do you really . . . 'see' things? Ahead?

Diana   I just look at the alignment of the stars, that's all. And suggest how that affects folks' moods. He asked me to look at the year ahead, actually, Mr Murdoch. For both of you. This place, the paper.

Lamb   I don't wanna know.

Diana   Fair enough. (*She's leaving.*)

Lamb   Diana . . .

Diana *stops.*

Lamb   Just out of curiosity, then.

Diana (*smiles*)   It ain't all up and up and up, Mr Lamb. It's like – well . . . it's like the *Sun*, isn't it? Sometimes up, sometimes down.

She goes, leaving **Lamb** *alone momentarily.*

The private back room of a Chinese restaurant on the Street.

A secret summit meeting of editors descending from their offices – **Cudlipp** *the ringleader.*

Cudlipp (*somewhat hushed*)   I'm telling you, it's the only way –

Hetherington   Christ, we couldn't have met in the Press Club? This place –

Cudlipp   – the only way, is to come together to defeat a common enemy.

Rees-Mogg   All this cloak-and-dagger stuff, it's unseemly, and comes about as close to establishing a mafia racket as I'm willing to abide.

Brittenden   It's the Dirty Digger running the racket –

Cudlipp   Yes!

Brittenden   There's been an understanding on this Street, for generations; we *don't* engage in distribution wars, and yet what has he done? Increased the percentage of the cover price he gives to the newsagents. A disgrace. Now guess which paper they're pushing hardest on the counter? – even my local shop. And I live in Queen's Park!

Cudlipp   So why then am I the only one whose voice is out there on the attack? We've got to present a united front, this is a war –

Hetherington   Oh Hugh, let's dial down the rhetoric, shall we –

Cudlipp   I'm serious –

Hetherington   – otherwise we end up bloody well sounding like his shit sheet, all capital letters and 144-point fonts – (*Louder.*) In A Permanent State of Exclamation!

The others shush him, as he picks up some Chinese nibbles.

At best it's a civil war, no more.

Cudlipp   They're the worst kind! Where we end up destroying one another when we should be rounding on them!

Hetherington (*gasps a little at his prawn ball*)   Ooh. Hot.

Brittenden   I can't pretend the rot isn't spreading, I mean, several hours this morning my senior editors and I spent discussing the merits of showing a small suggestion of . . . pubic hair, through the fabric of some new lingerie we shot.

Cudlipp   Pubi— Arthur!

Brittenden   When is a 'wisp' not a 'wisp', you tell me.

Rees-Mogg   I'm going to have to sit down.

Brittenden   We didn't, obviously, but that was my morning. How was yours.

Cudlipp   Finalising John Pilger's spread on the atrocities in Cambodia.

Hetherington You're lucky. I was rowing with an artist drawing cartoons to help illustrate a piece on erectile dysfunction in middle age.

Cudlipp Oh, God!

Hetherington I ordered them to take it down.

Cudlipp Good, spike the whole thing.

Hetherington Not the piece, the erection. I wanted it below, you know – (*With his hand.*) Forty degrees, but then we got into this big debate about to what degree higher or lower counts as an actual erection, I mean, *is* it one if it's below forty?

Brittenden Christ, one has to hope, these days.

They laugh a little, and then some more, the tension easing slightly. A sigh . . .

Hetherington God, look at us.

Rees-Mogg Can't you bring Larry to his senses, Hugh? He was your boy.

Cudlipp . . . No, he's . . . not any more. Listen. They can only win if we all follow, start to chase him downwards, into the gutter, but if we all take an oath now, I mean it, an oath together to, no matter what, avoid that temptation –

Rees-Mogg Well, Alastair – I'm not casting – but the *Guardian* broke ranks first –

Hetherington We're a liberal-leaning newspaper, and it's entirely different.

Rees-Mogg All this homosexuality and, and –

Hetherington Which is legal now, William; you're equating that with this?

Brittenden I can't hold back the wolves from my door much longer. The *Sun* are this close to passing the *Mail*, and my board are . . . As a broadsheet, well, we'll be a tabloid by the end of the year, and I'll be gone, you watch. Relief, in a way.

Cudlipp   No, no, not on my watch. We raise our voices, we can be louder than theirs. Help Me. And they will Not Win, I *swear it.*

They disperse, as the lights cut out, and a new headline appears above us:

PAGE TWO

Rules restaurant.

Murdoch *and* **Lamb** *at their table.* **Lamb** *has a collection of other papers he's going through.*

Lamb   One point two-six.

Murdoch   One point two-six?

Lamb   Million, readers, as of yesterday, we're about to overtake the *Mail.*

Murdoch (*offering his glass*)   Congratulations.

Lamb   Don't congratulate me yet, we're still three million behind the *Mirror.*

Murdoch   Yeah yeah, but you have to celebrate the battles on the way to winning the war?

Lamb   Winning? Oh have you not seen our reviews? (*Moving through the papers.*) 'They appear to have an obsession with the bizarre, the sexy, and the unpleasant' – *New Statesman.*

Murdoch   Which no bugger reads –

Lamb   'Mr Murdoch has not invented sex, but he does show a remarkable enthusiasm for its benefits to circulation' – *The Times.* And 'The clock of journalistic standards has been put back five to ten years' – surprise surprise, the *Mirror.*

Murdoch   The prattling classes who don't get it. So what?

Lamb   I just want you to be aware. That's all. There's been a shift, on the Street. A 'disruption', just as you asked for.

Murdoch   Wonderful.

Lamb   And I wanted you to know how rough it's getting.

Murdoch   How rough?

Lamb   'Historically' rough. The Stab in the Back has turned into a daily war zone between *Mirror* hacks and those who support them, which is many, and the *Sun* and those who support us, which is none. Chairs, fists, glasses. I've got fashion editors in catfights on the catwalks, sports writers being the ones pulled apart by referees, *that* fucking rough.

Murdoch   Haha! What did I tell you?! It was *there*, waiting to be awoken. All those things you buggers think of when you think of *us*, that we are, what, essentially – 'savage'. Well – (*Slams.*) Didn't I say? There's always been flashes of it – the football hooligan, the striking worker? Well, they can all shove that up their pipes and smoke it.

Lamb   We won't win properly until we win *them* (*the papers*), over, win the argument, that's all I'm saying.

Murdoch   Why do you care what they think? It unsettles me, this part of you that wants their acceptance. Makes me think you might not be willing to go all the way, do what has to be done.

Lamb   Excuse me and what transgressions have I not already willingly committed thus far, in pursuit of a goal I happen to believe in?

Murdoch   The old *Sun*, on its last day, sold just 650,000. You and your guys have taken it up to 1.2 million, in a month; a *month*. That has never happened before, anywhere on the planet. Who needs friends when you have readers? (*Laughs, drinks.*)

Your father would be proud, I'll bet.

Lamb   My father had friends. Lots of . . . 'Pillar of his community', not . . .

Murdoch   I don't like how you have drinks in your office with the senior staff at night, sends the wrong message. Too convivial, be better if they were scared of you.

Lamb   My team, are the reason we're doing so well, I asked them to step up and they did. Frank Nicklin, a pie-and-pint man, shot down *twice* in the war, he's writing sport like it's never been written before, like you're down the pub with the fellas, chatting. Bernard Shrimsley, son of a tailor who treats page layout like it's a Savile Row suit, has turned ugly into an art form. All of 'em, signed up to what we're doing. Why? Because they believe in it.

Murdoch   Good, I'm just saying, you need to stop worrying about being liked.

Lamb   Whereas that never even registers on your radar, does it.

Murdoch   Being liked? Why should it? I love – I bloody (*Fist on the table.*) Love, the amount of events Anna are I are *not* getting invited to now. It's thrilling.

Lamb   . . . So what is it, then? For you. What *does* Rupert Murdoch want?

Murdoch *continues to just tuck into his food, amused by the line of inquiry, smiling at* **Lamb**.

Lamb   Not riches. Attention. And not even 'friends', awww.

Murdoch   Awww, yeah no time, truth be told. Anyway, I like moving around, never in one place long enough. Isn't that the joy of a hotel? You can check in, turn it over, spill a glass of wine, take a shit in the toilet, fuck in the bed, make a mess and then leave. And someone else cleans it up after – isn't that wonderful?

It's all 'chip-wrapping' end of the day, right? You said that.

Lamb   Everything's discardable? Even this? (*Referencing them both.*) Am I just chip-wrapping, Rupert?

Murdoch   . . . Bugger off, you soft pom. If I *did* have any friends, you'd be the closest thing to it. And how fucking depressing is that.

Talk to me about Cudlipp. We should be expecting retaliation from the *Mirror*?

Lamb   All-out assault; they're launching a full-colour magazine, the first of its kind in the world.

Murdoch   Full-colour? Sounds expensive.

Lamb   I think we should be advertising on television.

Murdoch   Newspaper don't advertise on television.

Lamb   *You're* appearing on television –

Murdoch   That's different, that's –

Lamb   We could be the first. Television is not our rival. Our TV pages? Man alive, the market research says they're our most popular –

Murdoch   I know, I pay for the market research –

Lamb   It's the same audience, a *popular* audience.

Murdoch   Fine, advertise on television, but keep 'em cheap. Maximum impact, minimum length.

I wanted to talk about some – don't get precious, just some of the choices, on the themed weeks. This . . . the knickers thing last week. Anna didn't like it.

Lamb   She didn't like 'knickers week'?

Murdoch   It was the . . . what was it again?

Lamb   We gave away a load of knickers.

Murdoch   Why?

Lamb   Because it was 'knickers week'.

Murdoch   Why did we have to have a 'knickers week' in the first place?

Lamb   We didn't have to have a 'knickers week', no one has to have a 'knickers week'. If Anna —

Murdoch   No, it's not just Anna . . . *I'm* not a fan of it, truth be told.

Lamb   Why?

Murdoch   And with Anna being Catholic and, yes, truth be told, I find it a bit —

Lamb   Re–eally? Knickers, in a tin?

Murdoch   They were in a tin? A pair of ladies' . . . ?

Lamb   Yeah, anyone who sent back the voucher, we shoved them some knickers in a tin.

Murdoch   Why did they have to be in a tin?

Lamb   They didn't *have* to be in a — Stop saying 'have to', we 'chose' to. I can't believe you're squeamish about *this*, of all the . . . You told me to go to war by being the loudest, brashest — that's what you said, well that's what I'm doing.

Murdoch   Fine, I'm just passing on some feedback.

Lamb   We did spray them. With Chanel No. 5.

Murdoch   Chanel No. 5?

Lamb   Yeah you see, classy. Maybe Anna didn't sniff them.

Murdoch   I don't want my wife sniffing knickers in a tin. Why are you trying to make people sniff knickers in a tin?

Lamb   Because it was 'KNICKERS WEEK'! Fucking hell . . . (*Smiles.*)

How the tables turn, eh . . .

Murdoch   Nothing's turned, if it sells, do it, doesn't mean I always have to like it.

Lamb   It's about me getting us past the *Mirror*, Rupert. So let me do that.

Beat. Downs his drink and about to leave.

Murdoch   Just stay smart, OK?

Frank *at his typewriter, speaking as he writes, 'sport commentator' style.*

Frank   And now on to some results we don't often publish on these pages, but it's close to my heart – the *Sun* newspaper has *soared* ahead up the league table –

We might see a visual representation of a graph, with moving lines each representing the figures of the papers, racing each other like horses, with the Sun *gaining ground all the time (including a backdrop of some of their more shocking front pages, including* THE DAY OF THE MAD DOGS, *featuring a photo of rabid canines, foaming at the mouth . . .*

– passing the 1.5 million mark now, *surging* ahead of the *Guardian*, and look at this, overtaking the *Telegraph* on the outside, pulling away from all the 'unpopulars' as we call them, and now it's approaching the *Mail*! Is it going to pass it, YES! It's through –

Music, building in momentum, as –

Brian *sits watching a young actor,* **Christopher Timothy**, *reading some voice-over lines into a microphone, terribly well-spoken, as* **Lamb** *enters to listen.*

Christopher   That nice little woman down your street? Underneath it all she's one of the huntresses. This week, the *Sun* looks at a new breed of woman who no longer waits to be asked. Young and old, single and married, they all hunt their men and bring them back alive. Meet the huntresses, in the *Sun*.

Learn how to talk to your pussy and give it what it wants. It's Pussy Week in the *Sun*.

And let those truckers roll! Find out what it's like in the world of the truck drivers. Discover the secret of their private code, learn their slang and meet them. In 'Go Trucker Go'.

All in your 5p *Sun*, this week.

(*Looks.*) How's that?

Brian   It's still a little over, slot's thirty seconds and that was forty-one, we're going to have to make some cuts.

Lamb   No cuts, get him to speak faster.

Christopher   Do I keep having to say 'in the *Sun*' at the end of every line? I could just say it at the end.

Lamb   No, that's the most important bit – what's your name?

Christopher   Christopher, sir, Christopher Timothy, I'm an actor.

Lamb   Yeah, well, stop being an actor.

Christopher   Stop being an actor? I'm from the Old Vic.

Lamb   Be a, be a mate down the pub, cab driver pulling up at the lights and spotting some girls, be – you know – cheeky. 'Nudge nudge, wink wink, me old darling'.

Christopher   Oh I see, the old 'don't mind if I do' sort of fella.

Lamb   Exactly – (*Quietly to* **Brian**.) Are there no actually genuinely working-class actors you couldn't fucking find?

Brian   You would be surprised.

Lamb   OK, go again, in under thirty seconds, and louder, wake people up.

Christopher *goes again, at more of a lick, getting halfway through, before* –

Lamb   No, you're not going to make it, again, don't draw breath.

Christopher   Don't draw breath? Acting is all about the breath.

Lamb   I told you not to be an actor, and louder still.

Brian   Are you sure, boss, adverts are meant to be soothing and calm –

Lamb   Yeah, well, we're not selling bloody Hovis, we're selling . . . I don't know what, but go. Go!

Christopher *does it at a lick, again, it's quite impressive, and –*

Lamb/Brian   Yes!

Lamb   Well done, son, that'll hit them over the head, won't it? (*Handing him a sheet.*) Now squeeze this new line into it at the top.

Christopher   What?!

Lamb   Another promo we're adding in.

Christopher   But . . . ?

Lamb (*at* **Brian**)   If he draws breath, fire him.

He exits. **Christopher** *looks in mild horror at* **Brian***, who shrugs.*

Brian   You wanna mind him. See that scar? Legend is he was down the East End, Kray twins. He wanted some dirt on a story, they set the boys on him, lead pipe to the forehead, he went down, got up, wiped the blood off his face and asked them again. Repeated that cycle another four times before they eventually just told him.

Christopher *doesn't know what to say.* **Brian** *indicates he's recording again – go.*

Christopher   'This Week YOU become the TV critic win a trip to New York only in the *Sun* that nice little woman down your street, she's – '

At the Mirror. *A launch party, in front of all the* Mirror *staff.*

Cudlipp *holding up a new full-colour magazine.*

Cudlipp   We may be one of the oldest papers. But that doesn't mean we cannot innovate. The IPC are calling this the publishing innovation of the decade! Full-colour, a revolution in journalism, maintaining our reputation as the '*intelligent, quality tabloid*' that we are so proud to make. Thank you! All of you. Keep at it.

Applause. He steps into –

The editor's office at the Mirror.

Lee *is here, flicking through magazine.*

Lee   Looks expensive.

Cudlipp   Quality costs, it also pays. The focus groups love it. They can't believe it's free.

Lee   I can't believe it's free. Shouldn't we be advertising? On television?

Cudlipp   . . . Oh I see, like they are? No thank you –

Lee   Hugh, maybe just –

Cudlipp   I don't want to think about it, those adverts make my ears bleed. Like the paper makes your eyes bleed, it's making the country fucking bleed. No. What do we think their response will be?

Lee   Their response? 1 thought this was our response to *their* response, you think *they're* going to respond?

Cudlipp   Whatever happened to our 'eyes and cars' over there?

Lee   . . . It's getting a little – harder, some of . . . well a lot of them seem to have . . . 'turned'. I think they're starting to 'believe'. Hah. If you can believe that. (*Off* **Cudlipp***'s look.*) I'm on it.

Photo studio. **Beverley** *and* **Joyce** *with models* **Stephanie**, *dressed in provocative red outfit holding a red flag,* **Chrissie** *in blue holding a torch. All of them being marshalled by* **Bernard**.

Bernard   Right, Beverley will drive you all to Number 10 – now you're going to have to be quick, the bobbies will probably make you scarper pretty sharpish.

Beverley   'S alright, I've been practising, doesn't take me much time to shoot what I need these days.

Joyce   I'd keep that to yourself, dear. (*As* **Beverley** *goes.*) Where's the Liberal one?

Stephanie   Toilet, says the orange is unflattering, she's redoing her powder.

Chrissie   'Ere, we're not going to get arrested, are we?

Bernard   No, it's just a little bit of 'cheek'.

Stephanie   What do you think, Mrs Hopkins? About this stunt? All in good taste?

Joyce   . . . I think young women being confident in their own skin while making a fun political point is not necessarily a bad thing, Miss Rahn. So long as it's clever.

Bernard   Oh, it's very clever, it's illustrating the different election manifestos. (*At* **Stephanie**.) Labour. (*At* **Chrissie**.) Tory and – wherever the Liberal Party is.

Joyce   JESS! We're going!

Bernard   On the effect you intend to, uh, 'have', on our male readers. Lusty Labour, you want to give workers a . . . 'rise'. Tarty Tory hopes for some 'steady expansion'. And the Luscious Lib wants to guarantee our readers some 'growth'.

OK, I'm not saying it's 'Oscar Wilde clever', but it's 'Larry Lamb clever'.

Stephanie   This is his idea? He asked for us personally?

Joyce   Right, get in the van, tick-tock.

Stephanie (*going*)   And what are the other papers doing?

Bernard   Oh, probably just printing the pledges, word for word?

Joyce *and* **Chrissie** *are going,* **Stephanie** *hanging back momentarily with* **Bernard***.*

Stephanie   Least I'm Labour. Mum would have murdered me otherwise.

Bernard   Ah, young innocent lefties. It happens.

Stephanie   Lefty, I'm practically a communist. Speaking of which. You're the deputy editor right? How come Beverley and the other snappers get £10 for the hour whether it's an hour, twenty minutes or five, and yet we only get a tenner if we hit the hour otherwise it's deducted accordingly?

Bernard   Find a union, love, and join it.

Stephanie   Find the twentieth century, mate, and join that. (*Beat.*) I'm only saying . . . I read Mr Lamb's editor's notes. If he's actually for young people, and women, well . . . he should prove it closer to home.

Bernard   . . . I'll see what I can do.

They both depart.

Behind them – the Mirror*'s 1970 election front cover coming out for Labour, as usual.*

The Sun *headline, the morning after the vote: 'Well done, Ted Heath. The British love to see an outsider come surging up to pass the favourite!'*

The editor's office.

A **Bench Hand** *is bundled into the office with force by* **Brian** *and* **Ray Mills** *– who bangs the pipe on the desk, frightening the lad as he is held down on a chair.* **Lamb** *paces.*

Ray   How much are they paying you?

Bench Hand   I dunno what you mean. No one pays me – you pay me!

Ray   You're a double agent for the *Mirror* – (*Slams the pipe down.*) Fucking talk!

Bench Hand   Ah, please!

Lamb   Sam? It's Sam, right . . . ?

Bench Hand *nods.*

Lamb   We have a little problem, a consignment of a very popular book we're giving out called *The Sensuous Woman*. Now for some reason the authorities, who we know deem this material to be unsuitable for the poor little innocent members of the general public, received a tip-off about our shipment arriving into Heathrow, and have confiscated the entire batch. And we'd like to know who told 'em, so the next batch might slip through easy peasy lemon squeezy, right?

Bench Hand   And you reckon it's me – ?

Lamb   I think some of the cunts left over from Cudlipp – yeah, Cudlipp's Cunts, I like that – have been kept on the pay of the *Mirror* to where possible, when possible, Fuck Us Over.

Bench Hand   . . . Me mum told me to. She said it was good, to be wanted by two people, shows resourcefulness. And I like Mr Cudlipp, what he's done for me. (*Not caring now.*) I LIKE HIM!

Lamb   Get him out, you're done.

Ray *lifts him up, bundling him into the main body of the newsroom.*

Ray   Come on, time for your send-off, tradition – everyone?

Lamb (*following now*)   No, no banging out.

Brian   Woah, boss, just let him –

Ray (*to the assembled*)   Young fella here is off, and as per the Street's –

Lamb (*into the main space*)   No banging out, not for this one!

Brian   Boss –

Ray   Boss, you got to, it's tradition.

Lamb   He's a traitor! A saboteur. This is an example, right, let the word go out –

Ray   Mr Lamb! It doesn't matter what he may or may not have done –

Lamb   I mean it! No banging out, I want your arms up! In the air now! Not a single fist or knock or clang or I swear to God you'll all be joining him. This kid leaves to silence, right?! Everyone, arms in the air!

The others in the newsroom lift their arms up, **Ray** *and* **Brian** *exchanging glances, as the* **Bench Hand** *looks around, close to tears, and slinks off out of the room to silence . . .*

After a moment . . .

Lamb   Alright, back to it.

He returns into his private office, busying himself as **Brian** *follows.*

Brian   Larry, what the hell –

Lamb   What?

Brian   They're not the enemy, gotta keep people on side, we need / to –

Lamb   On side, fine, not taking the fucking piss, we're not here to make friends, Brian.

Brian   Well, that's one target we've definitely hit then.

He goes. **Lamb** *is alone.*

He takes out a bottle and pours himself a drink. Sits – in his own editor's chair.

He feels it out, as though it might still not feel comfortable yet. As –

Over in the editor's office at the Mirror.

Hugh Cudlipp *sits with his own drink, listening to some Schubert. 'Ave Maria', or equivalent.*

Lamb *senses him, spins on his chair. Looking over in his direction . . .*

Cudlipp *opens his eyes. He turns his own chair gently, to face* **Lamb**.

Almost as if they're watching each other, across the divide of the Street.

Lamb *gets back to work – looking through a series of photo proofs of models.*

Flash, flash, flash –

As **Stephanie Rahn** *appears – modelling for the camera in different poses while* **Lamb** *looks through the hard-copy snaps himself, one after the other.*

Suddenly –

Stephanie *is replaced, by* **Muriel McKay**.

Lamb *freezes. Holding up that single photo, curiously.*

Above us, we may see the actual photo of the real Muriel McKay, smiling for the camera.

When suddenly –

From the darkness, **Muriel McKay** *is grabbed and pulled into the shadows, screaming.*

Lamb *stands, recoiling back.*

The phone starts ringing. **Lamb** *staring at it. Before we snap into –*

The editor's office, morning.

Sir Alick *is there. Sitting, wrapped in his coat, shaken. A woman's handbag on his lap.*

Lamb   What happened, Alick?

Sir Alick   It doesn't make sense, it makes no sense, Larry –

Lamb   OK, it's OK, breathe, take a breath, here – (*He offers him a drink.*) Just give me the basics, the who, what, when and where's – *where* were you?

Sir Alick   Home, I got home.

Lamb   When?

Sir Alick   Usual time, I don't know, give or take.

Brian *rushes in, with* **Bernard** *close behind.*

Brian   Boss?

Lamb *holds his hand up – wait a sec, as* **Sir Alick** *continues.*

Sir Alick   7.45-ish? The door was off the, the thing, what's it called, on the –

Lamb   The what? The latch?

Sir Alick   No, the . . . you slide it across on the door, and –

Lamb   The chain.

Sir Alick   And the phone had been ripped off the, the wall, and her handbag with all her stuff, scattered across the kitchen floor, look –

He holds up a woman's compact.

A flash bulb –

An image of **Muriel McKay** *in the same office, powdering her face from Act One. Turning to* **Lamb** *and smiling. She disappears.*

Lamb   Who, though? Who would want to – is there anyone who might –

Sir Alick   Muriel? No, how can you even . . . unless it, it's me, they're . . . because of what *we're* . . . (*Looking at* **Lamb**.) What *you're* doing here, but why Muriel?!

Joyce *arrives, taking her coat off – everyone seems to have been called in late.*

Joyce   Muriel? She's . . .

Sir Alick   Oh Joyce –

They hold one another. **Frank** *and* **Beverley** *arrive too. Confused by the scene.*

Joyce   It'll be fine. She's a tough cookie, and there'll be a logical – something.

Brian   What did the police say, Alick?

Sir Alick   They said just wait, they're saying – (*To* **Lamb.**) They told me not to talk to you. They said make sure we don't publish anything –

Brian   Wimbledon, is it? I know the DS down there, let me get the – (*Picking up a phone.*)

Sir Alick   But we have to publish *something*, Larry, what are we now, we're . . . (*He stumbles to* **Lamb**'s *sales chart.*) . . . 1.7 million people?! Someone must know something –

Joyce   Larry, if the police are saying –

Brian (*on the phone*)   DS Smith, please; Brian McConnell.

Sir Alick   Just her photograph, and the number for the police. And for here! All those telephones, people can call in, with information. That's all, Larry. (*At his watch.*) I have to get back to the house, if someone calls, or if *she* comes home –

Lamb   Bri, look after Alick, and speak to the coppers at the scene, just to see if there's anything we can, I dunno . . .

Sir Alick *goes, followed by* **Brian**. *A moment . . .*

Lamb   Bernard, clear the front page tomorrow.

Bernard   Should we . . . ?

Lamb   What?

Bernard   Check with . . . Where's Mr Murdoch?

Lamb   Australia couple days, with Anna, and I don't need to check anything, clear it. The rest of you spike whatever you're doing, get on this.

Frank   . . . alright, boss. If that's what you want.

Everyone leaves. **Lamb** *picks up the phone, and dials . . .*

We hear **Murdoch***'s voice, on speaker . . .*

Murdoch (*voice only*)   Yes?

Lamb   It's Lamb.

Murdoch *appears in the office, as though the conversation were now happening face to face. They both pace, smoking.*

Murdoch   How is he?

Lamb   Yeah, he's − you know.

Lamb   We . . . we need to work out how to 'report'. This.

Murdoch   . . . Report it?

Lamb   Yeah, we're a newspaper, this is news. Alick asked, I'm not just being −

Murdoch   What— . . . whatever you think's best.

I should fly home.

Lamb   You don't have to, we've got this.

Murdoch   It's Alick.

Lamb   He's fine, he's got − everyone here, he's like family, he's −

Murdoch   Yeah, well, to me he *is* family. I'll finish here tomorrow. (*Tosses his fag.*) This is strange. What does it mean?

Lamb   Doesn't mean anything, it's just happening.

He steps into −

The newsroom − some of the senior team gathered around **Bernard***'s desk for the page layout.*

Bernard   Main picture of Muriel here, eight by six −

Lamb   Bigger, ten by eight –

Ray   Headline, width of the masthead: 'Mystery of Missing Muriel McKay'.

Lamb (*with a pencil*)   No one knows who 'Muriel McKay' is, need to start this story like everyone's a new character, come on – 'Press Chief's wife'.

Brian   I didn't think we necessarily wanted to, you know, make this about us.

Lamb   This is about us. It's happening to one of our own.

Blow up the information hotline to 122, and centre it there, thank you.

He steps into his office, **Brian** *following him in.*

Lamb   What did they say, the coppers?

Brian   . . . It's a kidnap, Larry. They telephoned in. Last night and . . . (*From his pad.*) Uh, and said 'Tell Mr McKay . . . that we have his wife. We tried to get Mr Murdoch's wife. But we couldn't get her. So we took yours. We want one million, by Wednesday night. Or we will kill her.'

Beat. **Lamb** *begins making notes – never not a reporter.*

Lamb   No other instructions? Where to drop the ransom, how?

Brian   No, listen, the police . . . They haven't dealt with a kidnap for ransom case in –

Lamb   Who, this particular branch?

Brian   *Any* police force in Britain. For eight hundred years.

Lamb (*puts his pencil down*)   . . . Fuuuck.

So if this wasn't happening, to one of our – then there's no question in hell we'd not be feeling it up like a drunk uncle at Christmas. And you, Jesus, the best crime writer on the Street, it's like your career has been one long build-up to –

Brian   No, the police – because there's no precedent, and no one knows what they're bloody doing, they're saying please, please, Larry, don't go getting involved.

Lamb   Well what do they know? They said they don't know what they're doing, we could – The more people that know about this the better, surely, that's common fucking –

Brian (*scribbling in his notepad*)   I, I, I'm, Larry –

Lamb   Brian. We've turned the British public into journalists, agony aunts and gossip columnists, may as well turn them into police investigators as well.

Brian *goes.*

Murdoch *appears again in the office, as though on the phone.*

Lamb   I'm sorry, you can't come home.

Murdoch   Why not?

Lamb   The people who did this, they weren't after Muriel. They were after Anna. This is about you. When you lent Alick your car, the Rolls, while you were away, they followed . . . they got the wrong house when they followed Alick home, and they . . .

Murdoch   Uh-uh . . .

Lamb   The advice from the police is – stay away.

Murdoch   No, bollocks, no bloody way, the other side of the world?! While this –

Lamb   It isn't safe –

Murdoch   While someone is doing *this*? To *us*! To my paper? No . . . (*He takes a breath, smokes.*) Shit, I fe— I feel something terrible, too awful to say.

Lamb   . . . I know, you're glad it wasn't you. Course. Anyone would think the same, I would. If Joan . . .

An indecipherable noise from **Murdoch**.

Lamb   Rupert, it's the biggest story we've ever had, we're going to lead with it again tomorrow, and a five-page spread.

Murdoch   Lead on it?

Lamb   An exclusive, I mean, fuck me sideways and backwards, this *changes* the very definition of 'exclusive'.

Murdoch   I'm not sure, something . . . I don't, it doesn't feel right.

Lamb   Doesn't feel right?

Murdoch   About this story, I don't know.

Lamb   We can't ignore the story, we *are* the story.

Murdoch   Yeah but . . . Yes, but –

Lamb   Monday's edition, the 'vanishing wife', it broke 1.8.

Murdoch (*smokes*)   How is he?

Lamb   How do you think?

Murdoch   Shitting fucking hell cunt Christ, is this . . . doesn't this feel too perfectly conceived as some like cruel bloody . . .

Lamb   What?

Murdoch   . . . Test.

(*Smokes.*) You couldn't write it, and if one of your guys had I wouldn't believe it.

Lamb   Well I guess that's what makes it such a good story, eh?

Murdoch   . . . Don't do anything stupid.

The newsroom, around **Bernard***'s layout desk.*

Brian   'The Five Day Mystery of Mrs Muriel McKay', centre page.

Lamb (*reading, half-mumbling*)   'Five days ago Alick McKay arrived home after a normal day at the office expecting to be greeted by his wife, but she was not there.' (*Making scribbles, handing back some copy to* **Ray**.) Jesus, can you get Barrie to punch it up a bit, reads like a school report not the crime of the century.

Bernard   This left sidebar you asked me to hold.

Lamb   Yes, let's ask the questions, one after the other, 'Why', 'Why', 'Why'.

Brian   Least important question, I always thought –

Lamb   To answer yes, but, not to ask. Why – haven't the kidnappers issued clear instructions on their demands. Why – is this the first such case in a century. Why – did they choose the McKays with a relatively modest fortune.

Brian   We know the answer to that one, they didn't.

Lamb   Yeh, *we* do, but they don't, do they?

'Some' of the process to build that page materialises in front of us: the typesetter punches his keys, the **Stone Hand** *hammers it with a mallet, the flong appears from the flames above us.*

Lamb *steps into his office, taking a drink and turning into* –

Lamb   What is it?

Diana (*has appeared*)   Don't want you thinking I'm crazy, it's just Sir Alick asked me if I knew anyone, who is known for this type of thing, like a psychic.

Lamb   Psychic.

Diana   Who's good at 'finding people'.

Lamb   You don't even believe in all that.

Diana   Well there is one, this Dutch fella who . . . it's weird, I know, but in the past, he's found people. Actually found them. It's a hellava fucking story if nothing else.

Lamb   . . . You told anyone, told Alick?

Diana   No, I came to you first.

She steps out, and we move into –

The newsroom.

Gerard Croiset *has arrived – a Dutch clairvoyant, a little surprised by the setting and attention.*

He's sitting facing **Sir Alick**. *The rest of the senior team are here –* **Lamb** *perched on his desk,* **Joyce**, **Frank**, **Diana**, **Ray** *and* **Brian** *standing sceptically on the periphery.*

Beverley *moves awkwardly around the space, trying to be discreet, kneeling down and taking photos, having been ordered to capture the moment.*

Gerard   I asked you for a photograph? Of Muriel?

Sir Alick   Yes –

He hands one to **Gerard**. **Beverley** *takes a flash photograph, kneeling nearby, with everyone half-glancing at him, half-pretending this isn't happening.*

Gerard   And a map of London?

Bernard   Um, here – (*Unfolding and presenting it to him.*)

Gerard *lays the map on his lap, and holds the picture in his hand.*

Beverley *takes another reluctant flash photo.*

Gerard (*closes his eyes*)   . . . It's white, where she is.

Sir Alick   White?

Gerard   A white building. A white – farmhouse. Somewhere in the country. (*With the map.*) Feels like . . . what is this area?

Ray   That's east of the City, there's nothing there really, just docklands.

Gerard   No, this has trees . . . (*Closes his eyes, feeling the map.*)
This is – North-East London. Definitely a farm.

Sir Alick *gasps, then tries to push it back in, reeling in his hope.*

Gerard   Near a disused aerodrome. (*Looks up.*) I can hear
planes, passing over . . .

Sir Alick   Muriel . . .

Brian (*with his pad*)   You've found people before. In Canada,
France?

Gerard   But a lot of it is chance, you know? I've been as many
times right as I have wrong. I don't / claim for a second . . .

Sir Alick   Here's another photo. The whole family . . .

Gerard (*takes it, holds it*)   Your children.

Sir Alick   Yes . . .

Gerard   Two daughters and a son –

Sir Alick   Ian, yes, and Jennifer and Diane –

Gerard   The thought of them. They give her such comfort.
Such strength.

Sir Alick   Oh . . .

Gerard   She's alive . . . (*Placing his hand on* **Alick***'s cheek.*)
She's alive and she loves you . . .

Alick *rests his face against his hand.*

Beverley *takes a quick picture, and then looks down, unable to look
anyone in the eye.*

Gerard   But if you don't find her . . . she'll be dead in
fourteen days.

Sir Alick   She'll . . . ?

Lamb   OK, I think we have enough, that's all.

Gerard (*being led by* **Brian**)   That's all?

Sir Alick (*standing, to* **Lamb**)   The police! We must tell the −

Lamb   We will, they'll know.

Sir Alick   She's *alive* . . .

He follows **Gerard** *out with* **Brian**.

Frank   Bloody nonsense, the lot of it.

Lamb   No different from her scopes every day.

Diana   Uh −

Frank   Can't print any of that, can you? Fucking deranged −

Lamb (*to* **Beverley**)   Run me off your top ten prints before lunchtime.

Beverly, *fiddling with his camera, nods, not saying anything.*

Lamb   What? . . . (*Seeing he's upset.*) Oh for fuck's sake, the lot of you.

He marches off, leaving the team, into −

His office.

Joyce (*holding a letter*)   We've received a complaint, brace yourself . . . from the actually fucking *kidnappers*.

Lamb (*snatching it*)   From the kidna— Complaining, to *us*?!

Joyce   They can never get through on the phones, they say, because it's always engaged. The number we gave out −

Lamb   Oh I'm sorry! Are we − ?! Is that our − ?!

Brian   And plenty more besides; hoax letters, fake ransoms, sending the police on wild goose chases, 'I think I saw Muriel McKay on the train from Ipswich to Felixstowe', we bloody ran that on page four, that's a couple of days the old bill won't get back. They're going spare, Larry −

Lamb   OK, OK, OK . . .

Joyce   And then there's this one, in particular.

Lamb (*taking the letter, reads*)   You don't show this to anyone –

Joyce   Obviously.

Lamb (*gesturing as they go*)   Go on.

They both leave. **Lamb** *picks up the phone . . .*

Murdoch *arrives.* **Lamb** *hands him the letter.*

Lamb   You got it?

Murdoch *paces, reading it, as though it might be a fax, or . . .*

Lamb   Police confirm it's a hoax, they have the bloke who sent it, some fella . . .

Murdoch   'I will let Mrs Mackay go, if the *Sun* publicly announces . . . that they will not corrupt our kids any more, by printing all that filth'.

OK . . .

Lamb   Like I say, it's fake.

Murdoch   But someone actually wrote it, it's real –

Lamb   Not the kidnappers, some nutcase –

Murdoch   But it's what people are thinking, out there –

Lamb   No, actually, 'people' can't get enough of –

Murdoch   But it's what people are *saying*, that we're in some way –

Lamb   We're in no way nothing, we didn't bloody take her, it's –

Murdoch   We should stop, shouldn't we? Shouldn't we stop?

Lamb   Stop? Stop what?

Murdoch   The story. We should kill it – not 'kill' it, I didn't mean, but –

Lamb   Why? Because it's happening to us? And you don't think that in any way smacks a little bit, Rupert, of slight double –

Murdoch   That isn't fair, and Larry, don't talk to me / like –

Lamb   Would you like me to read the mission statement we published on our first day, echoing your own words? 'Light into every corner, no matter how . . . into Normal People's lives, if it's what people want to read'? I'm sorry I must have missed the caveat that said 'everyone *except* when it concerns the *Sun* itself'!

Silence. **Lamb** *puts the phone down.*

Brian *appears, handing* **Lamb** *another letter* –

Brian   It's from *her*. It's the real deal. Alick's confirmed the handwriting.

Lamb   (*holding it*)   'Alick, darling. I'm blindfolded, and I'm cold . . . ' (*He stops, a moment. Continues.*) 'Please co-operate, or I can't keep going. Muriel.'

No one else has this?

Brian   Well the police have it –

Lamb   I mean no other . . . paper. (*Off* **Brian***'s look.*) Run it. Run it.

Brian *takes it and goes.*

Lamb *spins and leans against his desk, taking a breath. He necks a drink. Before turning into* –

The composing room, night.

Larry *facing off against the* **Chapel Father***, surrounded by his team* – **Brian, Joyce, Beverley** *and* **Diana** – *all standing by* **Ray** *at the stone.*

Lamb   They're not serious?

Ray   They're deadly serious, Chapel Father's calling a walk-out if you print that letter, I'm just the messenger, though personally –

Lamb   They're bloody / running it! What right –

Ray   My personal feelings are, are much the same.

Lamb   They'll do as they're paid to. I'm the editor. And this is my paper.

The reporters wrote it, they're happy with it, the typesetters set it, they're happy with it. The readers have proofed it, they're happy – happy, happy, happy, every step of the way, so why has it stopped here at the stone?

Ray   It took a while for the . . . the full scale of it to sink in.

Lamb   Get the Stone Hand, fetch him.

Ray   Stone Hand won't do it.

Lamb   Then find me someone else.

Ray   Larry, there –

Lamb   . Find me someone else!

Ray   It has to be a member –

Lamb   It doesn't have to be anything, they're walking out! Fine, they forfeit their rights, don't they? Find me someone else.

Ray (*looking at the others from the core team*)   Am I the only one? Really?

Beat. **Ray** *goes.* **Lamb** *paces, checking his watch, aware his team are watching him.*

Brian   Boss, maybe we should all just think about it, for a second –

Lamb   There isn't *time* to think about it. We want it out there, don't we, as much information as possible? Don't we?! It can *help* –

Ray *leads the shell-shocked* **Apprentice Printer** *in.* **Lamb** *grabs him by the arm and drags him to the stone.*

Lamb   Right, you – you're NGA aren't you?

Apprentice   RIRFA.

Lamb   Get this story moving – (*Hands him the mallet.*) Go on.

Apprentice (*staring at the mallet in his hand, and at the others*)
I can't –

Ray   Larry –

Lamb   Shut up – do it.

Apprentice   I know what this is . . . they're all talking
about it.

Lamb   Go on. (*Beat. Grabbing his arm.*) I said go on!

Apprentice   I won't!

Lamb *pushes the boy out the way and grabs the mallet himself.*

Brian   Oy! / Larry, come on!

Bernard   Mr Lamb!

Lamb   We agreed! In this room, we all signed up, or have
you forgotten?! Either we believe in this, or we don't! Either
we're right . . . or we Stop Now!

The team waver, looking at one another.

You fucking hypocrites . . .

Lamb *is glaring at them, and at the stone, the story, waiting . . .*

He raises his mallet –

*And begins to strike a blow, hard, down on to the stone. Again . . . and
again . . . ink splattering on to him as he keeps going, harder and faster,
harder and faster, harder and faster.*

The lights closing in around him . . .

We hear the voice of a **CID Commander** *being interviewed on
radio.*

C1D Commander   I believe that if news of Mrs McKay's disappearance had not been released so early we could have established a quick line with the kidnappers. We were embarrassed by the intensity of the publicity. It could be it forced the kidnappers beyond the point of no return. That is the question that will be posed for a long time.

Lamb *steps into his office.*

He's sitting, covered in ink. Still . . .

Murdoch *is back, staring coldly at* **Lamb***, still in last night's clothes.*

Beverley, **Frank**, **Joyce**, **Diana** *also here, along with* **Bernard***, just arrived, with his notepad.*

Lamb   . . . Welcome home, Rupert.

Murdoch (*to* **Bernard**)   Go on . . .

Bernard   I'm getting this second hand –

Murdoch   Go on.

Bernard   Early hours of the morning, police descended on Rook Farm, in Hertfordshire. A white farmhouse, north-east, of London . . . (*Flicking through his notes.*) Two brothers. Trinidad origins. Muslim. Arthur and Naz. There's no sign of any body yet, they're still searching, but –

Murdoch   What else?

Bernard   Alick is down the station now, with Brian for . . .

Murdoch   What else?

Bernard   This Naz fella. His wife. (*To* **Murdoch**.) She said they watched you.

The flicker of a TV monitor somewhere –

Murdoch*'s face, staring down the lens, in black-and-white . . .*

Bernard   On television. Was all he talked about for weeks, his desire to, quote, 'be something'. An outsider, prove himself. The locals started calling him 'King Hosein' . . .

(*Handing* **Lamb** *an article.*) We should prepare ourselves for some – backlash. Running in *The Times* tomorrow.

Lamb *looks, and then thrusts the article into* **Frank***'s hand, marching to his phone.*

Frank (*reading*)   'Did Publicity Help to Kill Muriel McKay?'

Lamb (*on the phone*)   Rees-Mogg, please?!

Bernard   Boss?

Lamb   No! They're gonna accuse us . . . (*On the phone.*) Well, find him then!

Murdoch (*snatching it from* **Frank**, *reading*)   'The kidnappers, kept aware of the search, every step of the way, in their own morning paper . . . '

Lamb (*on the phone*)   It's Larry Lamb, I want you to find him –

Murdoch   ' . . . The agonising question for Alick McKay is did his own newspaper reduce the chance of her being returned – alive.'

Lamb   Bullshit!

Sir Alick *enters the room, followed by* **Brian**.

Murdoch   Alick . . .

Sir Alick *looks at him, as* **Murdoch** *places a hand on his arm.* **Lamb** *puts the phone down.*

Sir Alick   Muriel . . .

Brian   They, uh, they've charged the two brothers.

Murdoch   So they . . . (*Holding* **Alick***'s arm.*) Have they found her?

Brian   . . . They think they – that they fed her to the pigs.

Silence.

Bernard *turns and vomits, aiming for the waste paper bin.* **Joyce** *puts up hands to her face.*

Sir Alick *walks forward, dream-like, towards* **Lamb***.*

Sir Alick   Larry . . . Did *we* . . . ?

He stumbles, and both **Murdoch** *and* **Lamb** *hold him.*

Murdoch   It's alright.

Sir Alick (*weeping*)   Rupert . . .

Murdoch   We've got you, mate, it's alright . . .

He slinks further to the ground, limp, and the two of them clumsily try to hold him up. The three of them together, as the man cries out.

Murdoch *and* **Lamb** *looking at one another, helpless . . .*

Sir Alick   Why? . . . My Muriel, why . . .

After a moment, he frees himself from **Lamb** *and* **Murdoch***, standing, newly angry, and goes to flip* **Lamb***'s desk in a rage.*

Only he can't lift the big heavy thing. Struggling.

Lamb   Alick –

Sir Alick   I just . . . just want to . . .

He struggles. **Lamb** *indicates to* **Murdoch** *and some of the others. They come to the desk and help him to lift it and slowly tip it over. Phones and papers scatter . . .*

Sir Alick *pants, out of breath, staring at them all.*

Before making his way slowly out.

Everyone but **Murdoch** *and* **Lamb** *follow him out.*

Brian *momentarily lingers on the threshold, looking back at* **Lamb***. He goes.*

Silence.

Lamb *goes to the board of strings, and raises the* Sun *even further.*

Getting ink on the board from his still messy fingers . . .

Murdoch   It's unthinkable. *Why?*

Lamb   There is no 'why'. Only – 'what next'?

The Schubert returns . . .

St Bride's Church.

Journalists and editors we recognise, arriving in black.

Sir Alick – *lost.* **Murdoch** *arrives with him. And they hold each other.*

Lamb *watches, some distance away. And* **Cudlipp** *watches him.*

Archive Radio (*voice-over*)   'St Bride's Church plays host to many events in the Fleet Street calendar. Weddings, baptisms. But occasionally, every so often, something more solemn, as today, the Street gathered to pay tribute to Mrs Muriel McKay . . . '

Lamb *wanders into the church alone, after the ceremony.*

Everyone else gone, as he sits.

Almost everyone . . .

Cudlipp   Would you like me to leave you alone?

Lamb   It's a church, innit. 'For everyone'. Private thoughts.

Cudlipp   Oh, so there's still the odd sacred place left, is there, free from the glare of publicity and attention?

Lamb   Wow, that is decent of you, Hugh, today of all days. If you're going to lecture me like you do your readers – look, there's a pulpit right there, at least do it properly.

Cudlipp (*hands up*)   I'm not here to – anything, I'm sorry.

I knew her, you know. Muriel McKay.

A moment . . . then, half-laughing, possibly even half-crying now, the exhaustion of it all . . .

I don't know what to do, Larry. The ground beneath me, it's like nothing is solid, any more.

I'm on the wrong side of history, aren't I?

Lamb   . . . No, course not, just –

Cudlipp (*pacing away*)   Oh, don't worry, doesn't matter, bloody hell, happens to all of us, that's the only reason I got into my chair in the first place, my predecessor, falling behind the times.

Lamb   You're still a million readers ahead, of everyone, I should be the one –

Cudlipp   Ha ha, and yet every day, chip, chip, chip –

Lamb   Only a couple of weeks left, until our first birthday. A year since we launched – he gave me a deadline, did you know that? To beat you, the *Mirror*. Just once, if only for one day. And we're closer, we are, thanks to . . .

Cudlipp (*referencing the wake*)   Thanks to 'this', yes. Yes, you came very close.

Lamb   You're a hypocrite; you chase circulation like anyone, chased it when I was there, you bloody invented the 'populist' tabloid, I just perfected it. You *had* them, the people. Had them and then forgot them.

Cudlipp   I didn't forget them, you took them. We were offering, I don't know – a diet of nutritious vegetables with *some* fresh pudding for afters, and you came along waving a packet of sweets, well –

Lamb   Oh Hugh, for pity's – people / aren't children, for –

Cudlipp   And yes I have some experience of 'populism',
Larry, from when I was on the right side of history – 1939?
The rest of the Street, desperate to reflect what 'real people'
thought, how many papers supported appeasement? Peace
with the Nazis – the Nazis who themselves had the popular
support of the mob. Playing to people's fears, their hatred, and
anger. Well *I* didn't. The *Mirror* didn't. Because who says the
'majority' is always right? Oh yes, sorry, so speaketh the elitist.
Well, ask an American a hundred years ago, they'd have said
that slavery was right; ask people in this country *now* and
they'll tell you they want the death penalty, are *they* right?

Lamb   Ah, so democracy, fine, so long as they're saying what
you want to hear. Well, I'm sorry you find it all so ugly, Hugh,
but the world is ugly.

Cudlipp   Oh, and you think we should just accept that?

Lamb   It's not that I 'accept' people at their worst! It's just
understanding that none of us are ever at our best!

We're all sinners . . . he knew that. Adam and Eve. Banished
from the garden, where we ran around. 'Naked, and Not
Ashamed.'

You turned the *Mirror* into a fig leaf, Hugh, hiding our true
selves in the dark.

Cudlipp   And what is your paper, then, Larry?

Lamb   . . . We're the *sun*.

He makes to leave. **Cudlipp** *grabs* **Lamb** *as he passes. Close,
now . . .*

Cudlipp   It doesn't have to be like this. One, or the other.
If we stop now. You get what you want. I get what I want. And
they get *some*, of what they want…

Lamb   . . . I can't. (*Moving away from him now.*) Can't stop now,
after –

He extricates him from **Cudlipp**, *stepping away.*

Cudlipp   And I won't give up either. So, what next?

Lamb   Buy tomorrow's paper, Hugh. Read all about it.

He goes.

The editor's office. **Lamb** *with* **Brian** – **Lamb** *at the figures. The gap between the lines.*

Lamb   That. (*At the gap.*) What – is – that, what would fill *that*, for fuck's –

Brian   In twenty-four hours, nothing. If a kidnap and murder story didn't get us there, the scoop of the fucking year, then nothing.

Lamb   (*snapping*)   Well then, they must want something else! Right? Or the gap wouldn't be there, would it?!

He steps away from **Brian**, *into* – **Diana**.

Lamb   Diana, I want you to fiddle with his star signs again, tomorrow. He's flown back to Oz to collect Anna, we need to delay him another day.

Diana   Delay him, how?

Lamb   I don't care, clouds over Mars, rumblings in Uranus. A massive fucking meteorite heading straight for the Sun . . . ?

He moves away from **Diana**, *into* – **Joyce**.

Joyce   I don't know what to say, I can't quite comprehend what you're asking.

Lamb   A girl, a normal girl. But could be a bit more than normal.

Joyce   I take, I do take my responsibility towards them / incredibly seriously –

Lamb   Look, it's up to her, her choice, isn't that what we're all about?

Joyce   I don't know, honestly, I think I may have lost track of / what we're –

Lamb   Just pick one and send her to me, now.

He steps into – **Beverley**.

Lamb   We'd have to keep it secret, only a few people would know.

And I'd need an answer now. (*Looking at his watch.*) Less than now.

Beverley   . . .You know, a few of the older snappers, they drink over the Tip, couple times a week, invite some of us newbies along, mainly to take the piss, you know, sort of initiation stuff, but I like it. One of 'em, been doing it for longer than I've been alive, been in Ireland a lot, the Troubles. And his hands are all burnt. 'Cause of the magnesium, in the flash powder; got me thinking . . . Imagine every picture, burning itself into your skin. Where that's what every picture *costs*. What would you choose, to capture, with that . . . ?

Lamb   . . . You put them at ease, Joyce says, the girls. They like you.

Beverley   I like them.

No brainer, really, isn't it?

So why are my hands shaking?

Stephanie *enters.*

Lamb   Stephanie? Is it?

Stephanie   Mr Lamb.

Lamb   Please.

They sit. Beat.

Would you like a drink?

Stephanie   I'm alright, thank you.

You have one, though. I mean obviously, I know you don't
need my permission.

Lamb   I'm alright.

How about a smoke, do you smoke?

Stephanie   I'm good.

Lamb   OK.

Beat.

I think I will have a drink, actually, if that's alright.

He pours himself a drink. Takes a sip. Silence.

You like working for us, here?

Stephanie   Yeah.

Lamb   You like the paper?

Stephanie   Yeah, it – it's funny.

Lamb   Has Mrs Hopkirk explained?

Stephanie   She sort of has. You want me for a shoot.
A special shoot. A glamour shoot. Only this time . . .

Well why don't you explain it to me, Mr Lamb.

Lamb   Well. We're looking for something to – celebrate, our
year, in business. And so . . .

No, we're not looking for something to celebrate our year in
business, Stephanie, I want to beat the sales figures for the
Mirror tomorrow.

That's it. That's what this is. And I'd like to use you to do that.
Which might be unfair, I don't . . . I don't even know any
more, but that's where we are, and we're grown-ups and we
can say no – you, you can say no.

Stephanie   The shoot.

Lamb   . . . The shoot would be a glamour shoot, yes, you've
done those before so . . . *sans* clothes.

Stephanie   Naked.

Lamb   Right. Only this time. This time we would *see* . . .
your – front. Your chest. We would see your chest. And that
would be a thing because, it's not something that a newspaper
. . . a family newspaper, has done before.

The idea is that – you are wearing your birthday suit. That's
how we would sell it.

And there will be some attention around it, and I want to,
have to check . . . what you think about that.

Beat.

How long have you been doing this?

Stephanie   Couple of years.

Lamb   And what do you – do your parents, what do they
think?

Stephanie   About what?

Lamb   About you – taking your clothes off.

Stephanie   Is that what you think this job is? Taking my
clothes off?

Lamb   No, no, just –

Stephanie   Olympic swimmers have to take their clothes off
to go to work, would you call Olympic swimming just 'taking
your clothes off'? It's what comes after that part of the job
that's the job, Mr Lamb.

Lamb   I understand. I'm sorry.

Stephanie   No, I'm only kidding, I do find it very easy
actually. I'm not saying it's not a thing, I'm just saying for
whatever reason . . . it's always sort of come naturally. If that
makes sense . . .

I'm not completely new to all this, world of showbiz or what-have-you, my dad was in film, a distributor. My mum . . . well she's retired now, I'm all she has.

Lamb   And, what do you think?

Stephanie   Will people say that it's porn?

Lamb   They might.

You might think of it as just an extension of what we do already. Some might even say, although this is slightly wishful thinking, but they might even say that it's art.

Stephanie   What's the difference between pornography and art?

Lamb   Arousal over beauty?

Stephanie   Can't you get aroused looking at the Venus de Milo? Or at David?

Lamb   Who's David – oh, David. Well. I imagine that you can, yes.

I suppose, that, when you're selling sex, what you're trying to do – it isn't important, i.e. to talk about anything, or say anything, or change anything. I imagine that's what art is, or what artists think it is, anyway. Adding to the gross value of humanity.

Stephanie   Aren't we trying to change something?

Lamb   We're trying to win. And that might by default change something.

Often my job is to convince people to do things, to say things, to tell us things, they wouldn't otherwise want to do, by convincing them that it might matter, and I don't want to do that with you, Ms Rahn. I think what we're doing here, is trying to sell more newspapers to people who like looking at, at tits, by showing them some, somewhere they've never seen them before. In the fullness of time, maybe that will become important, or political, or art. I honestly don't know. Or care.

And it's only fair that you know that. And that if it isn't you, it'll be someone else.

So there we are.

Silence.

Stephanie   I might have a fag after all, if that's OK.

Lamb *finds his cigarettes, leans forward, handing her one.*

He pops one in his own mouth, trying to get his lighter to work.

Stephanie *produces some matches, and walks over to him. Standing above him.*

She strikes a match, and lights his cigarette.

Lamb   . . . Thank you.

She sits back down, and lights her own.

They smoke.

Stephanie   Will it be 'funny'?

Lamb   . . . No. No, it won't be funny.

Beat.

Stephanie   Are you a dad, do you have − ?

Lamb   Yes?

Stephanie   What?

Lamb   Daughter.

Stephanie   Really?

Lamb   Yes.

Stephanie   How old?

Lamb   . . . She's fourteen.

Stephanie   In a few years' time, would you let *her* do this?

Lamb   . . . I'd let her do whatever she wanted to do −

Stephanie   But would you want her to?

Lamb   No.

Stephanie   Will you let her look? At the photo. Will you let her look at me?

Don't *you* want to look? Check that I'm what you're looking for.

Lamb   That won't be necessary –

Stephanie   Why not?

Lamb   Because, I don't – want to.

Stephanie   But you want other people to want to.

Lamb   I do . . . It's not that I want them to.

Stephanie (*beginning with her shirt buttons*)   I think you should.

Lamb   No –

Stephanie   I think you should have to –

Lamb   *No.*

She stops. Beat. He drinks . . .

Stephanie   How did you get that scar?

Lamb   My scar? . . . Well, take your pick, a fight with the Krays, falling through a plate-glass window, leaping in front of a speeding –

Stephanie   The truth.

Lamb   The truth?

I was nineteen, young copy boy at the *People*. You've seen them spikey things, on the desks, to 'spike' stories, shove copy on to them when they cut? I dropped my pencil once, bent down to pick it up, spike went straight into my forehead, right through. Impaled, frozen, couldn't move. They had to saw it off while I was stuck there, take me to hospital with half of it still stuck in my head.

Stephanie   So why does everyone think it was something else?

Lamb   People don't like to think things don't happen for no reason, Stephanie. People need stories.

Beat.

Stephanie   OK.

Lamb   OK.

Stephanie   I'll do it.

Lamb   . . . OK.

Stephanie   Tell me the story.

Pixel by pixel, piece by piece, the first Page Three page from the Sun, *on 17 November 1970, begins to materialise under the story.*

Lamb   Only a handful of people will know.

We see them, going through this process . . .

We will drive you out of the city. We can't do this, in our studio. No one must know it's happening. We take you to a field. Somewhere.

And you will take your clothes off. And a picture will be taken.

The picture will come back here. Where only I, and my deputy editor, will be responsible for the layout of the page.

By the time it hits the print-room floor, it will be too late to stop it.

In the composing room, the hot metal lava starts to flow.

Lamb *arrives, with* **Stephanie** *in tow, to watch the process . . .*

The plate materialises from the heat of the forgery . . .

The sound of the presses starting up again . . .

Morning.

Around the Street, different people opening up the Sun.

Marjorie, *in disgust.*

Rees-Mogg, *in horror.*

And **Cudlipp**. *Unreadable.*

A new headline from the darkness . . .

PAGE THREE

The editor's office.

Around the Sun *offices, phones begin to ring in fury. Different members from our team –* **Frank**, **Beverley** *and* **Bernard** *and so on – answer at their desks, receiving what might possibly be angry tirades on the other end of the line, as –*

Lights arrive on the Sun*'s editor's office. At first there is a silhouette of* **Stephanie**, *sitting on* **Lamb***'s, desk, hands around her knees, reflecting the image of the first page three girl shoot.*

Lamb *enters.*

Lamb   . . . What are you doing here?

Stephanie   No one stopped me. They couldn't, it was like no one wanted to look at me –

A phone rings near to **Lamb**, *he answers expectantly.*

Lamb   Lamb.

He listens to something possibly unpleasant, and just slams the phone down, moving to his desk.

Lamb   You can't be here, not today –

Stephanie   Oh yeah. It's your birthday isn't it, 'One today.' Happy birthday.

A phone rings somewhere in the office, it's answered. The receiver listens, casting a disapproving eye over to where **Lamb** *is in his office.*

Lamb   Look, Miss Rahn –

Stephanie   I wanted to know the end of the story.

Did it work? Did you get what you wanted . . . ?

Lamb (*beat; at his watch*)   I – don't know yet.

Stephanie   Clothes.

Lamb   . . .

Stephanie   You haven't changed your clothes. You've not been home, have you? Are you hiding, are people after you?

Lamb   . . .

A phone rings, he answers, and listens.

Fuck you and fuck off. (*Slams it down, smokes.*)

Stephanie   *I* was at home. I was on the kitchen table, when I came down for breakfast. My mum had me in her hands. People started knocking on the door. Telephoning. Some family . . . My school, they said I shouldn't bother –

Lamb   I'm sor—

Stephanie   I don't want your sorry, I know what I did.

It's only when you turn it. And see it. And see everyone else seeing it. On the street, the bus. See them toss you away on to the floor . . .

I didn't know where else to go.

Rupert Murdoch *enters, slamming the door closed. Beat.*

Murdoch   What have you done?

Oh my God, is this the girl? What's she doing here?

Stephanie   My name is Stephanie, you probably recognize me from page three of your newspaper.

She offers her hand. He doesn't take it, marching over to **Lamb**.

Murdoch   I've had the Press Association on to me, I've had Members of Parliament on to me, I've had lawyers on to me, I've had Mary FUCKING WHITEHOUSE on to me! When it comes to decisions like this, you do Not Exclude Me! Not when you are bringing down my fucking newspaper! You realise this plays exactly into their hands?! That we're nothing more than a pair of pornographers?!

Lamb   . . Just chip-wrapping. Remember. Something to throw away.

Stephanie   Excuse me?

Murdoch   Excuse *me*, can you leave us please?! −

Stephanie   Leave? How? This is my life, now; stay here, go somewhere else, doesn't matter. *I* can't throw this away. (*Studying* **Lamb**.) You too, probably, eh? That's weird, isn't it. To think after this, I'll go and we'll probably never see each other again but we're linked in this now. Handcuffed together, for all time. Isn't that funny.

Beat. The phone rings.

After a couple rings, **Lamb** *answers it.*

Lamb   Give them to me.

He writes some figures down on a pad.

He puts the phone down. Looks at **Murdoch**.

Murdoch   . . . I don't care, we won't survive this.

Lamb (*at* **Stephanie**)   Give me your hand.

Stephanie   . . .

Lamb   I said give me your hand.

She does.

He leads her to the wall. The charts.

'London and the South East'.

Together, they lift the yellow line of the Sun . . . *above the red line of the* Mirror.

A moment. **Murdoch** *slumps down in his chair.* **Lamb** *slumps down in his.*

Stephanie   . . . Congratulations.

She looks at **Lamb**. *And then at* **Murdoch**, *who for the first time in this exchange are now looking directly at each other . . .*

The editor's office at the Mirror.

Percy, **Lee** *and* **Cudlipp** . . .

Percy   It's just time, Hugh . . .

(*Tossing the* Mirror Magazine *on to the table.*) A nice idea, but it didn't work.

Not immediately, not tomorrow, but . . . you know, a phased retirement.

The incredible legacy you leave at the *Mirror* –

Cudlipp   I am the *Mirror*.

Percy   . . . And the board feels like it needs a change.

Lee   I don't know how I'll begin to fill your shoes. But – I'll try.

Cudlipp   This is it. You realise that, this is one of those moments, people look back on, and say, 'When was it, that it all fell away?' (*Pointing.*) This is it.

Percy   Hugh. You sold them the fucking paper in the first place . . .

Fifty years, we maintained that lead. It took him one year to destroy it. One year, and a pair of tits.

Lee   We'll throw you a party. It'll be 'fun'.

The lights close in around **Cudlipp** *as he enters the* Mirror *newsroom.*

The Mirror *journalists begin to bang him out. The noise building . . .*

Lamb *steps forward from the* Sun's *office. Looking at him.*

Cudlipp *with as much dignity as he can muster, against the sound of the banging, exits the stage . . .*

Rules Restaurant.

Murdoch *and* **Lamb** *eating in silence.*

Well, **Murdoch** *is eating. A bloody steak.* **Lamb** *is quiet.* **Murdoch** *referencing a paper.*

Murdoch   Don't feel bad. It's not personal, it's business.

Lamb (*taking up the paper*)   He brought me on to this Street.

Murdoch   The Street's time is up, forget it. The first house has toppled, it'll be like dominoes now, bang bang bang. Soon all that'll be left to remind us it was ever there are tombstones. 'Here lies'. Hah. (*Laughing.*) Ha ha, that's good. 'Here *lies*', fuck, ain't that the truth?

I've found a bit of land. In the East End, the docklands, currently nothing. Of course it would have to be phased in, slowly, bit by bit, under the radar.

I know, I know, the romantic, sentimental, Larry the Lamb will miss the bars, and the restaurants and the hangouts and the history. Don't worry. There will be (*half-singing*) 'always something there to remind you . . . '

He eats. **Lamb** *stares off.*

Lamb   What is it really, though? This Street. Sat between St Paul's, the Courts of Justice. Law to the left of us, God to our right. And we straddle it. Delicately. To what end . . . ?

Murdoch   What's wrong?

Lamb   Nothing.

Murdoch   What are you thinking about?

Lamb   Thinking about why.

Murdoch (*presses an imaginary buzzer, making the noise*)   Bzzz! There is no why, you've killed 'why', Larry, just as you'd hoped to. 'Why' was how they controlled things, wasn't it? It was the source of their power, convincing everyone there is an overarching . . . 'idea'. Churches. Schools. Trade unions! Newspapers. Well – 'why' is gone now, we're free to just ask who, what, where and when? Who you wanna screw? What do you wanna buy? Where do you wanna go? When do you wanna go there? People love it.

Your father would have loved it.

Lamb   . . . My father believed in a 'why'.

Murdoch   Well, I'm sure he'd have believed in our third page too. He was a man after all.

Lamb   . . . He was a good man.

Murdoch   We should start schmoozing the Tories, this new government.

Lamb   . . . Our readers, working-class Labour –

Murdoch   Call 'em in, bite to eat. Not Heath, enough to kill your appetite, Jesus. I mean Joseph, and what's-her-face, that impressive bird in Education, get her in too.

Lamb   We have a problem, a lot of my team, they're . . . moving on.

Murdoch   So? Hire some more. Train 'em up, get 'em in, get 'em out.

I'll be sort of moving on myself, temporarily, actually. Or –

Lamb   You're what?

Murdoch   Looking at expanding. England's too small.

You know, it's strange. That . . . the whole, terrible, business, with the . . . Sir Alick. That really got people's attention. Far and wide. America, New York.

Lamb   New York?

Murdoch   I'm thinking about buying a TV network over there. TV is the future. You taught me that.

Lamb (*smiles, nods*)   You're going alone.

Murdoch   What, you mean you? I need you here, so much more to be done.

Lamb   Turning over the hotel room, eh? Cleaning up the mess?

Murdoch   . . . Larry.

Lamb   Do you ever think about her?

Murdoch (*beat; takes a sip of his wine*)   Who? Alick's . . . ? Course I do –

Lamb   I meant the girl. The *first* girl. Christ, there's been so many more since, every day, a roll call of . . .

I suppose I stupidly thought I could control it. Close the box, after that once. But . . .

Murdoch   Well, what can you do, people like it.

Lamb   You don't. You don't, Rupert, you can't even bear to look at it.

Beat. He takes out the day's paper and tosses it gently on to **Murdoch**'s *plate.* **Murdoch** *stops.*

Lamb   Look at it.

Murdoch   . . . I look at it every day. Every page.

(*At his watch.*) Nearly time for me to fly away –

Lamb   I'm stuck with it, aren't I?

. . . She was right. That'll be on *my* tombstone. My obituary, even, in the *Sun*! My own paper, how funny. Eh, if you live long enough you might even edit it yourself. Why do I feel like you probably will just somehow outlive us all?

Murdoch   . . .

Lamb   What will it say, I wonder, a life's work. What's the headline?

A flash of the Sun's *obituary of its own originating editor, Larry Lamb.*

Larry Lamb, the man who gave the world Page Three . . .

And we see others – the Guardian, *BBC, and yes, the* Mirror, *all headlines opening with Page Three.*

Murdoch   It's a good story, Larry. People like stories . . .

He wipes his mouth, winks, and exits.

Lamb *is alone. He pours himself a glass, and drinks. Above him some new headlines are typed.*

IN 1971 – THE DAILY MAIL FOLLOWED
THE SUN AND BECAME A TABLOID NEWSPAPER.
OTHERS QUICKLY FOLLOWED SUIT

IN 1975 – THE MIRROR 'GAVE IN', AND PUBLISHED
ITS FIRST EVER NIPPLE. NAKED MODELS
FOLLOWED SOON AFTER

IN 1978 – THE SUN BECAME THE BEST-SELLING
NEWSPAPER IN THE WORLD

IN 1989, RUPERT MURDOCH FINALLY FULFILLED
HIS DREAM OF TAKING THE PRESS OUT OF
FLEET STREET. HE ESTABLISHED A 'FORTRESS'
IN WAPPING THAT REMAINS TO THIS DAY

THE LAST NEWSPAPER LEFT THE STREET IN 2016

PAGE THREE REMAINS A FEATURE OF THE SUN
TO THIS DAY

Blackout.

For a complete listing of Bloomsbury
Methuen Drama titles, visit:
www.bloomsbury.com/drama

Follow us on Twitter and keep up to date
with our news and publications
@MethuenDrama